# MANAGING PROJECTS

# How To Books on business and management

Arranging Insurance
Be a Freelance Sales Agent
Buy & Run a Shop
Buy & Run a Small Hotel
Buying a Personal Computer
Cash from Your Computer
Collecting a Debt
Communicate at Work
Conducting Effective Interviews
Conducting Effective Negotiations
Conducting Staff Appraisals
Coping with Self Assessment
Counsel People at Work
Dealing with Your Bank
Delivering Customer Service
Doing Business Abroad
Do Your Own Advertising
Do Your Own PR
Employ & Manage Staff
Investing in People
Investing in Stocks & Shares
Keep Business Accounts
Manage a Sales Team
Manage an Office
Manage Computers at Work
Manage People at Work
Managing Budgets & Cash Flows
Managing Credit

Managing Meetings
Managing Projects
Managing Yourself
Market Yourself
Master Public Speaking
Mastering Book-Keeping
Mastering Business English
Organising Effective Training
Preparing a Business Plan
Publish a Book
Publish a Newsletter
Sell Your Business
Selling into Japan
Setting Up Your Own Limited Company
Start a Business from Home
Start Your Own Business
Starting to Manage
Successful Mail Order Marketing
Taking on Staff
Understand Finance at Work
Using the Internet
Winning Presentations
Write a Press Release
Write & Sell Computer Software
Writing a Report
Writing Business Letters
Your Own Business in Europe

*Other titles in preparation*

The How To Series now contains more than 200 titles in the following
  categories:

Business Basics
Family Reference
Jobs & Careers
Living & Working Abroad

Mind & Body
Student Handbooks
Successful Writing

Please send for a free copy of the latest catalogue for full details
(see back cover for address).

BUSINESS BASICS

# MANAGING PROJECTS

How to plan, implement and
achieve specific objectives

**James Chalmers**

How To Books

Also written by James Chalmers
*Organising Effective Training*

Cartoons by Mike Flanagan

**British Library Cataloguing in Publication Data**
A catalogue record for this book is available from the British Library.

First published in 1997 by How To Books Ltd, 3 Newtec Place,
Magdalen Road, Oxford OX4 1RE, United Kingdom.
Tel: (01865) 793806. Fax: (01865) 248780.

*Note:* The material contained in this book is set out in good faith for
general guidance and no liability can be accepted for loss or expense
incurred as a result of relying in particular circumstances on statements
made in the book. Technical and legal matters are complex and liable to
change, and readers should check the current position with the relevant
authorities before making personal arrangements.

Produced for How To Books by Deer Park Productions.
Typeset by PDQ Typesetting, Stoke-on-Trent, Staffs.
Printed and bound by Cromwell Press, Broughton Gifford, Melksham,
Wiltshire.

# Contents

List of illustrations   7

Preface   9

**1 Introducing projects**   11

Defining what a project is   11
Using project management to achieve results   12
Meeting the objectives   13
Clarifying the steps   16
Summary of key points   18
Case studies   19
Discussion points   21

**2 Making a good start**   22

Impressing the client   22
Building up the case   23
Branching out with a case study   26
Calling up the team   30
Looking at different team options   35
Meeting the project team   36
Recording the information   37
Summing up the case study   39
Summary of key points   39
Case studies   40
Discussion points   42

**3 Planning what needs to be done**   43

Taking the first steps   43
Breaking down the work details   45
Estimating the cost   51
Obtaining financial authority   53
Establishing dependencies   56
Summing up the case study   59
Summary of key points   59
Case studies   60
Discussion points   62

**4   Finding critical paths**                              64

Analysing the network                                  64
Unravelling the mysteries of CPA                       66
Plotting the paths                                     71
Summing up Critical Path Analysis (CPA)                77
Charting project activities                            78
Optimising resources                                   81
Summing up project planning                            82
Exhibiting success                                     84
Summary of key points                                  84
Case studies                                           85
Discussion points                                      86

**5   Monitoring the work**                              87

Keeping the project under control                      87
Measuring progress                                     89
Taking appropriate action                              92
Keeping the work on track                              93
Managing change                                        99
Summary of key points                                  103
Case studies                                           103
Discussion points                                      105

**6   Employing a computer**                             106

Assisting the project manager                          106
Using Project Management software                      108
Training yourself to use software                      111
Choosing your software                                 111
Shopping checklist                                     113
Case studies                                           114
Discussion points                                      116

**7   Finishing off the work**                           117

Closing the project                                    117
Learning for the future                                118
Recording the results                                  119
Filing project paperwork                               121
Summary of key points                                  123
Case studies                                           125
Checklist                                              126

Glossary                                               127
Further reading                                        130
Useful addresses                                       131
Index                                                  132

# List of Illustrations

| | | |
|---|---|---|
| 1. | Flowchart for customer service centre project | 14 |
| 2. | The relationship between time, cost and quality | 15 |
| 3. | The project life cycle | 17 |
| 4. | Project Manager selection score card | 24 |
| 5. | Railway project (start point) | 27 |
| 6. | Railway project (end point) | 29 |
| 7. | Client's requirements for case study project | 31 |
| 8. | Project team structures | 34 |
| 9. | Project team meeting agenda | 37 |
| 10. | Typical project file contents | 38 |
| 11. | A project activity checklist | 44 |
| 12. | The office move project | 46 |
| 13. | Office move work breakdown structure | 48 |
| 14. | Activity list for the office move | 49 |
| 15. | An alternative work breakdown structure | 50 |
| 16. | Cost estimate form for office move | 52 |
| 17. | Process for obtaining financial authority | 54 |
| 18. | The office move dependency table | 57 |
| 19. | The office move network diagram | 58 |
| 20. | The standard activity box for CPA | 65 |
| 21. | Exhibition dependency table and calendar | 68 |
| 22. | CPA network – activities and durations | 70 |
| 23. | CPA network – the forward pass | 72 |
| 24. | CPA network – the backward pass | 74 |
| 25. | CPA network – total float and critical path | 76 |
| 26. | Gantt chart for the exhibition | 79 |
| 27. | The project planning process | 83 |
| 28. | The project monitor and control process | 88 |
| 29. | Project reporting frequencies and methods | 90 |
| 30. | Example form for monthly progress reporting | 91 |

31. The children's farm case study　　　　　　　　　　94
32. The Gantt chart for the children's farm　　　　　　96
33. The children's farm project progress log　　　　　98
34. The project change process　　　　　　　　　　　100
35. A distribution list for controlling project documents　102
36. Gantt chart using typical Project Management software　110
37. A project closure report　　　　　　　　　　　　122
38. A project review report　　　　　　　　　　　　124

# Preface

We are living in a world of rapid change, so a reliable method of implementing change is essential. Project Management is highly effective for this purpose, because it delivers measurable benefits through specific objectives.

In this book, many different examples are used, to illustrate the various aspects of Project Management. There is also guidance on using computer software to assist the Project Manager.

Project Management is a useful addition to your other more traditional management skills. So good luck with your efforts, and remember, it only takes a bit of practice to acquire the ability to manage projects of any size or complexity.

*James Chalmers*

# IS THIS YOU?

Project Manager

Charity action group                                        Designer

Project Management consultant

Software engineer                                Project team member

Computer system designer

Architect                                                Civil engineer

Company director

Road planner                                                   Builder

Private utilities manager

Town planner                               Local authority planner

Local authority works department manager

Private railway director                          School headteacher

Customer service centre manager

University manager                               Personnel manager

Bank planning department manager

Health trust manager                              Marine engineer

Transport company manager

Museum director                                      Boat builder

Building society planning department manager

Entertainment manager                                  Hotel owner

Religious order

# 1
# Introducing Projects

## DEFINING WHAT A PROJECT IS

A project can be something quite simple and inexpensive, like erecting a garden shed. Projects can also be very complex and costly, for example, sending a man to the moon and getting him safely home again.

A project is:

**Work undertaken to achieve a specific objective.**

### Meeting the right criteria

For work to be a project, it must meet the following criteria. The project will:

- deliver a specified requirement or set of requirements to a client

- require a number of related activities to complete it

- require a team of people to complete it

- have a definite start and end point

- be a one off rather than repetitive work.

The last point is important. The production of building bricks in a factory, where bricks are routinely turned out, does not need Project Management. But a new housing estate, built from these bricks, would greatly benefit from Project Management.

*Exercise*
Test the criteria list by thinking about what each point means in relation to building a new housing estate.

### Ensuring effective Project Management

Let us now look at the basic nuts and bolts of Project Management.

There are three main contributors to managing projects effectively. These are listed below, with examples to illustrate each of the main areas. The term Critical Path Analysis, used as an example, may be new to you, but it will be fully explained in a subsequent chapter.

*The contributors to effective Project Management*
- **skills**, *eg*      – knowledge of Project Management
                    – experience of previous projects

- **tools**, *eg*      – pen and paper
                    – personal computer

- **methods**, *eg*      – Critical Path Analysis
                    – computer software.

*Tools*, such as computers, and *methods*, such as Critical Path Analysis, assist the Project Manager and the team to come up with the right answers. Project Management is logical and straightforward, and the advantages of using it can be very significant.

A key point to remember:

**Successful projects are delivered by people.**

## USING PROJECT MANAGEMENT TO ACHIEVE RESULTS

We undertake Project Management to deliver a benefit or improvement. Here are some examples of where Project Management would ensure the objectives are achieved:

1. reducing the running costs of a garden centre

2 increasing the revenue from racecourse entrance charges

3. raising the efficiency of farm milk production

4. improving the public's perception of the local police force.

Whatever the project undertaken, the criteria listed at the start of this chapter must all apply. You can test the examples given above, against these criteria, to check they would all be valid projects.

### Holding the gains
Once a project has been completed, and the benefits or improvements achieved, normal day-to-day operations need to take over.

An example is illustrated in Figure 1. The project is to create a customer service centre for a local authority, for enquiries on a freephone number, about anything from refuse collection to council tax payments.

The start point is an empty factory unit. The project will be finished, and have reached its end point, when the centre is operational and taking calls from customers.

When the project has delivered the operational customer service centre, the normal day-to-day process of running it takes over, and the project is closed.

## Programming a number of projects

Large organisations may need to divide their business initiatives into a number of separate but interrelated projects. A number of linked projects is called a **programme**. Here is an example:

**Programme:**
**To improve Haychester inner city sixth form education**

Project 1. Closure of facilities at St Mark's Comprehensive School

Project 2. Building of study centre at derelict dockland warehouse

Project 3. Conversion of Mill Street building for accommodation of overseas students

Project 4. Recruitment and retraining of specialist teaching staff

The whole inner city sixth form education programme could be tackled as one very large project, but it is much more manageable by being divided into smaller projects.

Each project will have:

- a separate budget

- a leader who has skills and understanding of the work involved

- team members who are directly involved with their own work area.

These three key points can be used to help a company decide how to divide a programme of work into separate projects.

## MEETING THE OBJECTIVES

The overall objective of a project has three key elements: **time, cost** and **quality**. Their relationship is illustrated by the diagram in Figure 2.

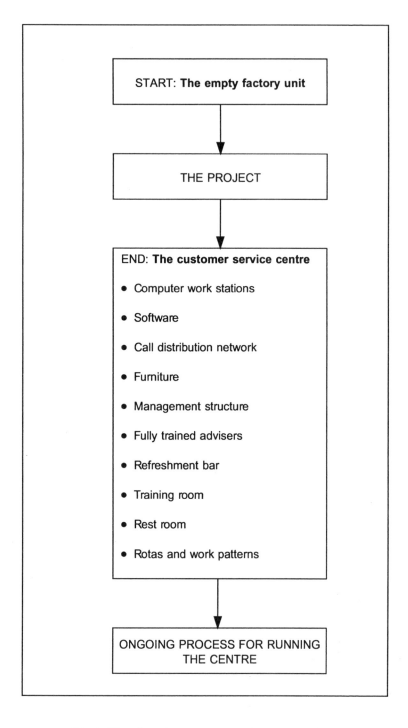

Fig. 1. Flowchart for customer service centre project.

Fig. 2. The relationship between time, cost and quality.

## Clarifying the meaning of quality

Before we examine how the three elements of time, cost and quality work together, we need to be clear what is meant by **quality**.

---

**The quality of a product, or the outcome of a project, is:
fitness for purpose.**

---

Another way of saying 'fitness for purpose', is to say: **fully meets customer expectations**.

To help clarify this definition, here are examples of two quality products:

Gold fountain pen – *looks nice and is very reliable.*

Plastic ball point – *cheap to buy and writes smoothly.*

In both cases the purchasers of these pens will be happy with the quality because their expectations have been met. The same applies to projects. The outcome of a project needs to match customer expectations.

## Dealing with time, cost and quality

The aim of all projects is to meet customer expectations. Here is what this means for the three key elements:

*Time*    – finished by agreed date
*Cost*    – completed within agreed budget
*Quality* – fit for purpose.

The triangle illustrated in Figure 2 represents the links between the elements. If one is changed then it is likely to affect the other two. This means that projects can fail to deliver the promised benefits, if a change to one of the elements occurs during the project, or there is an initial miscalculation. Here are some examples of how time, cost and quality interrelate:

1.  The director of a building company demands an earlier completion date for a housing estate.

    The work will cost more to complete.

2.  A civil engineering company is half-way through building a bridge, when the client insists on a higher specification for the steel.

    The work will cost more and take longer to finish.

3.  Budget cuts restrict the amount of money available for a children's playground being built in a local park.

    It is not possible to put a fence around it to keep out dogs. (This outcome is a reduction in quality.)

Effective Project Management, as described in this book, will allow you to avoid these difficulties, or to take appropriate corrective action, should things start to go wrong once the project has started.

## CLARIFYING THE STEPS

The period between the **start** and **end** of a project, is called **the project life cycle**. The life cycle consists of four stages. These are illustrated in Figure 3.

### Dividing up the life cycle

Before we look at the importance of the different costs of the life cycle stages, let us see what each stage means for our example of the local authority customer service centre project:

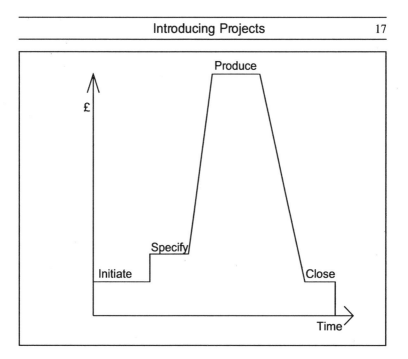

Fig. 3. The project life cycle.

**Initiate**      – Understand the requirements
Look at all the options available
*Building plans*
*Sketches of centre layout*
*Cost estimates*

**Specify**       – Define how the project will be delivered
When, by whom and at what cost
*The project plan which will show all the items that*
*have to be installed and ready and by when*

**Produce**       – The work is being done
Keep it on track
*Installation of equipment*
*Staff and management training*

**Close**         – Check that benefits have been achieved
Formally close project
*Measure how centre is operating for one month after*
*it opens*

You may feel a little uncertain as to what sort of items should be dealt with by the **Initiate stage** and which are part of the **Specify stage**.

In the example of the customer service centre, where they are moving into an empty factory unit, building plans are available from the estate agent, but the local authority's plans for the centre are just ideas sketched out on pads of paper. All of this goes into the **Initiate stage.** The detailed layout plans for the centre will be drawn up properly as one of the activities in the **Specify stage**.

Every project is unique and likely to be different from others previously tackled, but what is important in all projects is that *everything* about the project is known before moving into the **Produce stage**.

### Adding up the cost

Referring to the graph of the project life cycle, illustrated in Figure 3, you will see that the greatest cost of a project occurs during the **Produce stage**. This is why it is important to get things right in the first two stages, because the cost of these is relatively low.

Here is an example of how the customer service centre project could end up costing more, as a result of poor planning in the Specify stage:

–   Installation of the suspended floor takes three weeks longer than planned.
–   The engineers can't start putting the cables in until the floor is finished.
–   When the floor is finished, the engineers need to work a lot of overtime to get the project back on track.
–   The high cost of overtime payments was not anticipated in the original budget.

> **Spend time planning properly in the Specify stage,
> and you won't overspend in the Produce stage.**

### SUMMARY OF KEY POINTS

### Criteria for work to be a project
1.   Delivers specific requirements to customer.
2.   Consists of related activities.
3.   Completed by a team of people.

4.  Has a start and end point.
5.  Is a one off.

## Contributors to running a project
1.  Skills.
2.  Tools.
3.  Methods.

## At the end of a project
1.  Measure achievement.
2.  Normal process takes over.
3.  Project is closed.

## Use a programme of separate projects
1.  For large amounts of complex work.
2.  Separate budget for each.
3.  Individual project managers.
4.  Team members in their own work areas.

## The project objective consists of
1.  Time.
2.  Cost.
3.  Quality.

## The project life cycle stages
1.  Initiate.
2.  Specify.
3.  Produce.
4.  Close.

## Project costs
1.  Greatest in Produce stage.
2.  Plan properly in the Specify stage to keep control of cost.

## CASE STUDIES

### Norman's castle flies the flag
Norman, a history lecturer at the local university, has built his own
house in the style of a twelfth-century castle tower. The start of the
project was a derelict patch of land on the edge of town, and an idea
sketched in Norman's notebook. The end of the project was when
he hoisted the Union Jack on the flagpole above the mock

battlements. His friend, Tim, a maths lecturer at the same university, project-managed the work on Norman's behalf. The house was completed on time, at the cost originally estimated, and exactly as Norman wanted it.

### A change of clothes right on time
The Perrydown Building Society has merged with the large Midvale. The merger was project-managed once the shareholders had voted to accept the terms of the takeover.

The end point of the project was at 9.30 am on Monday 3 August. The Perrydown customer database had been transferred to the Midvale central computer. All the Perrydown branches had been reassigned to Midvale. The former Perrydown staff were fully trained for Midvale procedures, and were wearing Midvale corporate clothing.

The merger had to be completed to strict time and quality objectives, and the shareholders would have been reluctant to give authority for any additional budget, had there been a problem during the merger. The merger could not have achieved its objectives, without the use of expert Project Management.

### Lorry firm gets back on the right road
Westhoyle Transport has serious problems. It used to be a profitable road haulage company, but it is now losing a lot of its business to rival firms. If something is not done, then Westhoyle is certain to go out of business before too long.

The directors have approved a programme of work to tackle each of the problem areas. The programme includes a project to improve the company's image. This involves the scrapping of four of the older lorries, and repainting the existing fleet. A vehicle washing bay is installed at the main garage, and instructions issued to drivers to keep their vehicles spotless. The drivers have also been issued with new jackets, bearing the company logo.

The outcome is that members of the public and other drivers on the road are now seeing Westhoyle as a company that cares about its image. This project, although only one in the programme, makes a significant contribution to a large increase in the company's profits over the next twelve months, not only saving it from closing, but allowing it to expand.

## DISCUSSION POINTS

1.  Think about a task you have recently completed at home; for example, installing a fish pond, erecting a garden shed, or cooking a meal for important guests. Does the task fit the criteria for being a project? Can you identify the four stages as illustrated in Figure 3.

2.  In the building society merger case study, the formal project start was immediately after the vote at the shareholders' meeting. If you had been given the job to project-manage the merger, would you have waited until the outcome of the vote before initiating the project?

## 2
## Making a Good Start

**IMPRESSING THE CLIENT**

Projects have specific objectives. For example, a company has erected large signs on its headquarters building, so its name can be read by people travelling on the nearby railway. There was a single objective in this case – to improve the advertising of the company.

Projects always have a client – the person who says: 'This is what I want.' In other words, the person who sets the objectives.

### Clarifying the client's role
Sometimes a project may also have a customer. Let's look at examples of two different situations, to clarify who is the **client** and who is the **customer**.

*Internal project*
To introduce late night opening on Thursdays at the City Art Gallery and Museum.

Client: Gallery Director

*External project*
To repair the interior of the Parish Church Hall, using council work experience employees.

Client:    Leader of the District Council
Customer: Vicar of the Parish Church

*Notes*:
For projects run within an organisation or company there is just the **client**.

For projects run for someone who is not employed by the company, the **client** is a nominated person within the company who speaks on behalf of the external **customer**.

The **client** is the company representative for projects in all cases. So to avoid confusion, from now on we shall only refer to the client.

## Defining the client's responsibilities

In the two examples above, the client is the person who will set the objectives, because he or she works for the company managing the project.

The client has the following responsibilities. He or she:

- sets and agrees the objectives and other project requirements

- is responsible to the company for the success of the project

- gives or obtains financial authority for the project.

## Sizing up the Project Manager

The Project Manager is the person who runs the project, delivering the objectives to the client. A Project Manager can be:

1. a permanent job within a company to handle a wide range of regular project work, *or*

2. a person designated as a Project Manager for the duration of a specific project, possibly in addition to their normal duties, *or*

3. sometimes a consultant brought in from a specialist Project Management company.

## Profiling the Project Manager

The tools and methods described in this book are used universally in projects of all sizes and costs. Most people should be able to manage a project just as effectively as a permanently employed Project Manager. The only difference will be that the less experienced Project Manager may take a little longer over the planning stages.

A score card to help with the selection of a suitable person for the job of Project Manager is illustrated in Figure 4.

## Developing a person

Managing a project is an excellent opportunity for personal development at work. So don't overlook those who are less experienced but have potential for higher duties.

## BUILDING UP THE CASE

The Project Manager runs the project. The client therefore needs to give the Project Manager all the necessary details of what is required.

Score from 1 to 5 for each of the competences, inserting numbers in boxes, to rate the person you are thinking of selecting. Use the notes under each heading as guidance.

Score values: 1. poor             2. below average      3. average
                  4. above average  5. excellent

Nominee name: _____ is a/an:

☐ **Communicator**
Can explain what needs to be done, clearly and logically.
Can impart understanding of complex situations to non-experts.

☐ **Observer**
Likes to see what's going on for himself/herself.
Listens and takes into account the opinions of others.

☐ **Organiser**
Good with paperwork, including distribution of information, keeping things up to date, filing and general housekeeping.

☐ **Person able to cope with difficulties**
Able to take setbacks and difficulties in his or her stride. A *that's near enough* attitude is not compatible with effective Project Management.

☐ **Person able to work with figures**
Able to do simple maths: addition, subtraction, multiplication and division.

☐ **Computer operator**
Able to work with a personal computer, particularly for larger projects. Mark an inexperienced person a little higher if you think they would improve after suitable training. But mark lower for people who spend a lot of time talking about and playing with computers. In Project Management computers are tools not toys.

*Overall score*
Add up score in boxes to obtain a total.

10 or less      – unsuitable
19 to 23        – possible
24 and above – a wise choice.

Reject a candidate who scores 1 in any of the competences, however high their overall score is.

Fig. 4. Project Manager selection score card.

## Setting out the client's requirements

The client's requirements are set out formally as follows:

*Objectives*
- Why the project is to be undertaken.
- The benefits that will arise.

*Scope*
- What the project includes and does not include.

*Deliverables*
- The tangible outputs from the project.

*Related projects*
Other projects that depend on this project.
Other projects that this project is dependent on.

*Constraints*
- The conditions under which the project must be managed.

*Assumptions*
- Assumptions that have a direct impact on the project.

You can use this as a standard format for all your projects. Later in this chapter, we will look at a practical example, using a case study. But before that, it would be helpful to understand when the cost of a project is calculated.

## Estimating the cost

The client may give an estimate of how much the project is to cost, as part of the client's requirements. But it is usually not possible to provide a realistic cost until detailed plans are drawn up.

The accuracy of cost estimates depends on how and when the calculations are done. Here is a list of different types of estimates.

*1. Ballpark estimates*
Made before the Specify stage. Before many of the details of the work to be done are known.

- Accuracy is about + /- 25 per cent.

*2. Comparative estimates*

Can be calculated before the Specify stage. This is carried out by comparing work to be done on the new project with work done on a similar project in the past.

• Accuracy is about +/- 15 per cent.

*3. Feasibility estimates*

These are done after a significant amount of project planning has taken place. Provisional layouts and drawings are submitted to suppliers for quotations. The suppliers then do the estimating of the cost of materials and work.

• Accuracy is about +/- 10 per cent.

*4. Definitive estimates*

These are produced by updating the comparative or feasibility estimates on a regular basis, as the project progresses. A cost estimate should only be stated as definitive when it is known that:

• Accuracy is better than +/- 5 per cent.

**Publishing costing policy**

Companies who regularly undertake projects can use these estimate titles, and set their own accuracy limits, based on experience. This information should be published as company policy. Anyone in the company who gets involved in projects will then have a clear understanding of what the estimated costs mean.

**BRANCHING OUT WITH A CASE STUDY**

Let us now use a case study to see how a client specifies his requirements. This project involves the extension of the Hadlow Branch Line Railway (HBLR).

**Studying the history**

The HBLR was built in the last century, running from its junction with the main line at Ness Park Station, to the small country town of Hadlow. It was ten miles long, a single track with passing loops at Hadlow Town, and at Hoyle Bank, the one intermediate station. The railway operated passenger trains and some freight, mainly coal.

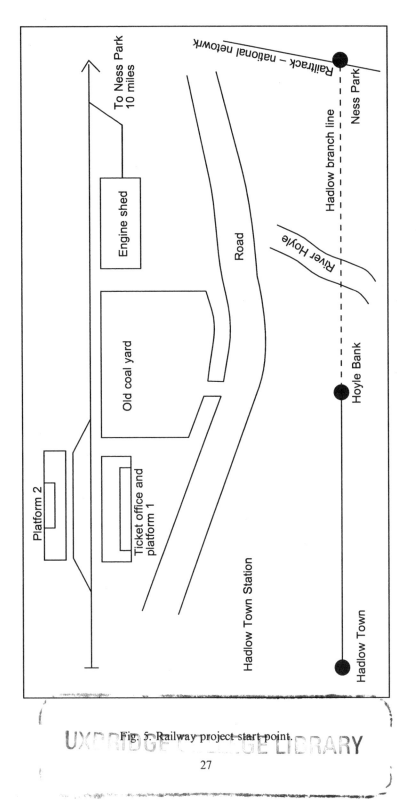

Fig. 5. Railway project start point.

The branch line was closed in the 1960s, but was reopened in 1975 by local railway enthusiasts. It then took ten years to get five miles of track relaid, and to start carrying paying passengers. The current situation, and the **start** point of the project, is illustrated in Figure 5.

## Going all the way

The HBLR currently operates as a tourist attraction. The new director, Major David Mitchell-Jones, the only full-time paid employee, wants to change the role of the HBLR, by reopening it all the way through to Ness Park and making other substantial improvements.

The work will include:

1.   laying track from Hoyle Bank to Ness Park

2.   building a new station alongside the county show ground

3.   creating a car park in the old coal yard

4.   building a new engine maintenance shed

5.   converting existing engine shed into a heritage centre and hostel accommodation for volunteer workers

6.   replacing missing signal box as an additional visitor attraction

7.   buying two additional locomotives, one diesel and one steam, to supplement the diesel and steam locomotives already there.

This all adds up to the situation illustrated in Figure 6. This will be the project **end point**.

## Programming the work

The replacement signal box, item 6, does not affect the running of the railway because it is to be just an additional tourist attraction. So this can be dealt with separately. Similarly, the heritage centre and the new engine shed, items 4 and 5, are not essential to the overall aim of getting trains through to the end of the line.

So rather than just one large project, the client decides on a programme of three separate projects. For the purposes of the case study, we shall follow the main project – the extension of the railway to Ness Park.

## Appointing the Project Manager

To manage the line extension project, the client, Major David

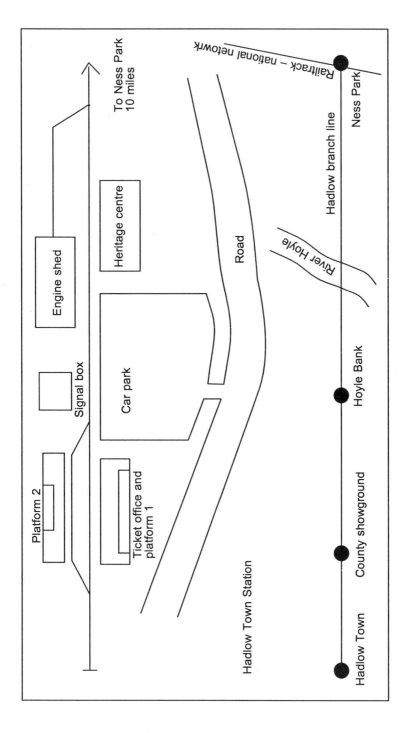

Fig. 6. Railway project end point.

Mitchell-Jones, appoints the following person as the Project
Manager:

Name              –    Laura Smith.

Employment        –    Hoyle District Council Service Centre
                       Manager.

Work at HBLR      –    Unpaid volunteer. Hadlow Town Station
                       Manager.

Personal profile  –    Good at explaining things.
                  –    Understands other people's points of view.
                  –    Station office is tidy and well organised.
                  –    Always stays calm if things go wrong.
                  –    8 GCSEs including maths.
                  –    Uses a personal computer at home.
                  –    Has completed a two-day project manager's
                       course at work.

### Setting out the requirements
The client's requirements for a project should always be written
down. The client's requirements for the line extension project are
illustrated in Figure 7.

### Talking to the client
The client's requirements are very important, because they tell the
Project Manager all he or she needs to know about the project to be
managed. However, what is more important, for *all* projects, is the
relationship between the client and the Project Manager.
    The client and the Project Manager must:

• talk to each other regularly

• listen to the other person's point of view

• be prepared to change their position if there is a good case to do so.

## CALLING UP THE TEAM

The **Specify** and **Produce** stages of a project are undertaken by a
team of people. But each project is unique, so the size and make-up
of the team will be different in each case. Let us look at who is
involved:

**Title:**
HBLR Line Extension

**Client:**
David Mitchell-Jones – Railway Director

**Project manager:**
Laura Smith

**Objectives:**
To run the HBLR as a commercial and profitable railway.
To carry commuter passengers as well as tourists.
To ensure the long-term survival of the railway.
To provide some paid staff jobs.
To generate money for the shareholders.
To reward the unpaid volunteers with a more interesting railway.

**Scope:**
This project includes track laying, acquisition of additional
locomotives, car parking facilities at Hadlow Town, and the
building of a new station at the county showground.
    This project does not include reopening of platform facilities at
Ness Park Station, which will be the responsibility of Railtrack.

**Deliverables:**
Half-hourly service with two trains, between Hadlow Town and
Ness Park. Diesel locomotives for commuter traffic. Steam for
tourist periods. Free car parking at Hadlow Town. Service to new
station at county showground.

**Related projects:**
Two related projects. Both non-dependent. Signal box and engine
shed/heritage centre at Hadlow Town.

**Constraints:**
Passenger service to be ready for 150th anniversary celebration of
the county show.

**Assumptions:**
Railtrack co-operation at Ness Park Station.
Hoyle Bridge will pass safety inspection.
Ballpark cost estimate for project is £1.5million. Half to be raised by
share issue. Half will be in grants and donations.

Fig. 7. Client's requirements for case study project.

*The Project Manager*
The Project Manager leads the team, may also plan much of the detail, and is responsible for ensuring the project is completed. For some projects, the Project Manager may do some of the work.

*Project team members*
Project team members report to the Project Manager. Their roles will include:

- directing others not on the team, to do part of the project work, *ie* acting as **supervisors**

- assisting the Project Manager with planning the project details

- doing some of the project work, *ie* acting as **workers**.

*Subcontractors*
Subcontractors are people who are not part of the project team, but who undertake part of the project work. Subcontractors can be people who work for the company, and who take on work as directed by members of the project team. Or they can be people who are not employed by the company, but who have been contracted by the company to do part of the work.

## Making up a project team
In practice a project team will consist of a combination of:

- Project Manager
- supervisors
- workers.

For very small projects, the team could consist of just the Project Manager; for example, reorganising the office filing system. Or it could be very large, involving dozens of people within a company, each with their own part to play.

*Key points*
1.  Avoid the project organisation becoming the driver. It should exist for the good of the project objectives. The project should not exist in order to justify a lot of meetings and free lunches.

2.  The Project Manager decides the size and make-up of the team, as well as the following issues:

- who will supervise
- who will plan
- who will do the work
- how often the team needs to meet formally.

3.  Each project is unique and will require a different size and make-up of team – there is no formula that can be used.

## Forming the Branch Line Team

Let us see what kind of team our case study Project Manager, Laura Smith, will have to help her with the project to extend the Hadlow Branch Line Railway.

*Finance, accounts and legal matters*

| | |
|---|---|
| Harold Yarbury | – retired accountant |
| | – works on the railway as a fireman |
| | – will be the link between the project team and the company's accountants and solicitors |
| Mott and Bailey | – local firm of accountants |
| | – not part of project team (subcontractors) |
| Burt-Shillinglaw | – local solicitors |
| | – not part of project team (subcontractors) |

*Engineering and construction*

| | |
|---|---|
| Hamish McFadyen | – head of county council highways maintenance department |
| | – drives HBLR engines at weekends |
| | – will act as link between project team and engineering subcontractors |
| EW Construction | – track and signalling engineers |
| | – subcontractors who will lay the track to Ness Park Station |
| Build-Best Ltd | – building company |
| | – subcontractors who will build the station at the county show ground |

*Purchasing/procurement*

| | |
|---|---|
| Jayne Farrington | – local shop manager |
| | – runs weekend café at Hadlow Town Station |
| | – will have responsibility for finding and purchasing the diesel and steam locomotives |

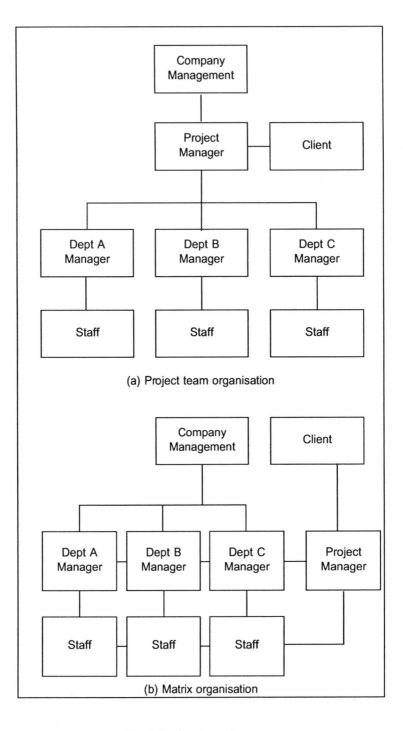

(a) Project team organisation

(b) Matrix organisation

Fig. 8. Project team structures.

*Hadlow Town Station improvements*

Philip Fines           – a former manager in the chemical industry
                         before taking early retirement
                       – in charge of locomotive maintenance
                       – will choose a suitable subcontractor for the
                         car-park work
                       – will organise a team of volunteers to repaint
                         the stations at Hadlow Town and Hoyle
                         Bank

*Note*

The subcontractors to lay the track and build the station at the
county show ground have been selected, prior to any detailed
planning. The railway already uses these two companies on a
regular basis and is aware of their quality of workmanship. But the
subcontractor to sort out the car park will be selected as part of the
planning stage of the project.

## LOOKING AT DIFFERENT TEAM OPTIONS

The way a project team is put together should be tailored to the
requirements of the project. This means having a flexible approach
in mind, and not getting bogged down by rigid theories about team
structures. You may, however, hear the more experienced project
people referring to different ways in which project teams can be
organised. Let us have a brief look at these, in order to clarify what
they mean.

The two different structures are illustrated in Figure 8.

### Project team organisation

In this arrangement, the Project Manager is given authority by
direct command over all departments involved in the project. This is
suitable for companies who are in business to run projects; for
example, the building industry.

### Matrix organisation

In the matrix arrangement, the Project Manager is allocated people
from different departments. The people on the project team have a
responsibility to the Project Manager for project work, but they are
still managed by their line manager in the normal way. This
arrangement is often used when making changes within a company,
where the changes affect a number of different departments.

## MEETING THE PROJECT TEAM

Regular meetings of the project team are essential. In the case study, the team members meet once a week in the lounge bar of The Railway Tavern to review progress.

### Structuring project meetings

Project team meetings can have different names, such as:

– Project Team Meeting
– Project Review Meeting
– Project Management Board Meeting

The essential features of a project meeting, whatever it is called, are as follows:

- The Project Manager decides if meetings are necessary, and how often they take place.

- Meetings are chaired by the Project Manager.

- There is a set agenda.

- A record is taken of discussion points and decisions, in the form of notes or minutes.

- Meetings are to the point – not just talking shops.

If the Project Manager decides not to hold regular meetings, then an alternative progress reporting method will be required. We will be looking at the details of monitoring the progress of a project in a later chapter.

### Drawing up an agenda

An agenda always helps to keep a meeting to the point and to time. The project team meeting agenda for the case study, the railway extension project, is illustrated in Figure 9.

*Hint for Any Other Business*

To prevent the Any Other Business (AOB) section from becoming a talking shop, the Project Manager should ask during his opening remarks if anyone is intending to raise any AOB items. These are then noted at the start of the meeting for discussion later. No further items are allowed to be introduced during any part of the meeting. This will limit the discussion to important AOB items, and cut out the trivia.

**Project Team Meeting Agenda**

**HBLR Extension**

24 May 20:30 hrs

Lounge Bar Railway Tavern, Hadlow

| | |
|---|---|
| 1. Any apologies for absence | 20:30 |
| 2. Project Manager's opening remarks and overview of progress | 20:35 |
| 3. Agree minutes of previous meeting and review action points | 20:40 |
| 4. Progress reports from individual team members | 21:10 |
| 5. Any other business | 21:50 |
| 6. Close | 22:00 |

Fig. 9. Project team meeting agenda.

## RECORDING THE INFORMATION

All projects should have a file of information. This will consist of either paperwork or a computer-based equivalent.

Project file key points are as follows:

- owned and controlled by the Project Manager
- should be set up at the start of the project
- initial contents will be minimal
- evolves and grows through to the close of the project
- can be used as reference material for future similar projects.

A suggested contents list for a project file is illustrated in Figure 10.

1. **Title page**
- Project reference number
- Company name
- Project title

2. **Distribution list**
- List of people who hold complete copies or relevant parts of project file

3. **Client's requirements**
- Objectives
- Scope
- Deliverables
- Related projects
- Constraints
- Assumptions

4. **Organisation and responsibilities**
- Project team details
- Subcontractor details

5. **Authorisation**
- Cost estimates
- Business case/cost benefits
- Authorisation signatures

6. **Plans**
- Work breakdown structure
- Dependency tables/activity durations
- CPA network
- Gantt chart

7. **Monitoring and control**
- Project reports
- Progress log
- Minutes of project team meetings
- Change requests
- Change authorisation

8. **Closure and review**
- Closure report
- Project review

Fig. 10. Typical project file contents.

## SUMMING UP THE CASE STUDY

In the case study, the Hadlow Branch Line Railway extension was opened on time, thanks to effective Project Management. However, before work started on laying the track, the Hoyle Bridge was surveyed and found to need additional strengthening.

The client met with the three Project Managers involved with the overall programme of work, and the decision was taken to stop the signal box project. This released sufficient additional funds to allow the bridge work to be done.

> **In Project Management, sometimes it is necessary
> to take hard decisions.**

## SUMMARY OF KEY POINTS

### The client
1.  Sets the client's requirements
    – objectives
    – scope
    – deliverables
    – related projects
    – constraints
    – assumptions.
2.  Is responsible for the success of the project.
3.  Gives or obtains financial authority.

### The Project Manager
1.  Manages the project for the client.
2.  Delivers the objectives.
3.  Can be a permanent position within a company.
4.  Can be appointed just for one project.
5.  He or she should be:
    – a good communicator
    – a good observer
    – a good organiser
    – good at coping with difficulties
    – able to do simple maths
    – computer literate or able to be trained.
6.  Giving someone the position of Project Manager is valuable for their personal development.
7.  A good relationship between the Project Manager and the client is very important.

## Cost estimation

1. The accuracy of cost estimation depends on when and how it is done:
   - Ballpark +/- 25 per cent
   - Comparative +/- 15 per cent
   - Feasibility +/- 10 per cent
   - Definitive +/- 5 per cent
2. Companies should publish their costing policy so that it is understood by all those involved in project work.

## The project team

1. Exists for the good of the project.
2. Make-up is decided by the Project Manager.
3. Each project will need a different kind of team.
4. Team will consist of:
   - Project Manager
   - supervisors
   - workers.
5. There can be subcontractors not on the team:
   - who are employed by the company
   - who are external to the company.
6. The project team may hold regular meetings to plan the work and monitor progress:
   - chaired by the Project Manager
   - using a set agenda
   - with records kept in notes or minutes.

## Project file

Each project should have a file of information:
- controlled by the Project Manager
- set up at the start of the project
- which evolves and grows as the project progresses.

## CASE STUDIES

### A lesson in Project Management

The Denhal High School has the highest truancy rate in the county, a reputation for violence against teachers, and some of the worst GCSE results in the country.

The local education authority director demands that something be done to improve the situation, and he sets tough targets of zero truancy and violence, and a 60 per cent improvement in GCSE results, all to be achieved within 10 months. If these targets are not met, the school is likely to close and most of the staff made redundant.

The existing headmaster is given early retirement, and an acting head, Darren Davies, brought in from a nearby business school. Darren, who teaches Project Management as one of his specialist subjects, takes on the role of Project Manager to sort out the school's problems.

A project team is formed, with representatives from each of the school's departments. However, all school staff are required to do their bit, as directed by the representatives who act as supervisors for the project work.

The project team meets weekly, with Darren not only leading, but teaching the team members how to effectively manage projects in order to achieve desired objectives.

The teaching staff on the project team find the subject new and interesting, and the project itself challenging. At the end of the 10-month period, the school achieves its targets and is saved from closure.

## Joe reins in some gold

The manager of the Western Woods Chalet Village Holiday Centre wants a rock and roll band to play 1960s revival music in the night club during the summer season. But he has been unable to find a suitable band, and the holiday season is only three months away. He passes the problem over to his entertainments manager, Joe.

Joe decides to create his own band, assisted by Project Management techniques. The starting point is to ask the centre manager to draw up a description of exactly what kind of band he wants, including number of members, type of instruments, style of music, and fees that will be payable.

Joe takes on the dual role of Project Manager and team member, but he does subcontract the work of locating suitable musicians to several agents. The final selection is made with the help of Joe's wife and some friends who are present at the auditions.

The band, called 'Reining Gold', is formed one month ahead of the start of the holiday season, which allows plenty of time for rehearsals. The client is pleased with the way the band performs, and even more pleased when they prove very popular with the residents, and the bar sales increase by 50 per cent.

**Professional approach solves pedestrian problem**
At the same time as the Hadlow Branch Line Railway is being extended, there are plans to pedestrianise Hadlow town centre.

The local authority has five permanent Project Managers, and one of them, Suzanne, is allocated to this project.

To achieve the project objectives, a number of different departments need to be involved. There is an inner ring road to be constructed, traffic flows changed on a number of the existing routes, new traffic signals installed, street lighting upgraded, trees planted, and the high street paved over.

Suzanne creates a project team, consisting of managers from each of the main departments involved. This is a **matrix** organisation, with the team members under Suzanne's control for the project, but still being managed on a day-to-day basis by their own managers.

With this arrangement, each team member is a specialist in their own work area, and they are still directly involved with their own people, maintaining motivation and morale.

Conscious that the nearby railway project is being run by part-timers, Suzanne takes great care with the management of her project, and as a result she achieves a successful outcome.

**DISCUSSION POINTS**

1. Projects can go wrong in the early stages as a result of problems, such as: client requirements not properly defined, long-winded project team meetings, inadequate records kept. How can these potential difficulties be avoided? How important is it to have the right kind of person as the Project Manager?

2. In the case study about the extension of the railway, the subcontractors laying the track and building the new station were chosen before much of the detailed planning had been done. What kind of cost estimates do you think would be used: comparative, feasibility, or a mixture of both?

3. Imagine you are a Project Manager in a large company. The senior managers have asked to be on the distribution lists for the project files of all company projects. Why is it important for you not to send them copies of complete files, but selected sections? Which parts do you think would be the most appropriate?

# 3
# Planning What Needs to be Done

## TAKING THE FIRST STEPS

In this chapter, we will be looking at how to identify all the work that needs to be done, to ensure the project meets its objectives. This is the first step in detailed project planning, and is part of the **Specify stage**.

The illustration of the project life cycle in Figure 3 shows that the cost of this stage of the project is relatively low, so it is important to get the planning right, to avoid costly mistakes in the **Produce stage**.

### Proceeding with care

Project planning techniques are logical and straightforward. They are used in exactly the same way for small, medium and large projects. Only a simple case study will be used in this chapter, but the methods could equally well be applied to a much more complex situation – for example, building a military aircraft.

The key points for successful planning are as follows:

- Take time to identify all the work that will be required, using the proper process – don't rush to produce a final list.

- Avoid going into a lot of detail in the early stages – for example, you will need to know that doors in a new office need painting, but don't worry about the colour.

- Sleep on your initial assumptions – come back later to consider if anything has been missed.

- Discuss your ideas with the project team, a friend or colleague – don't keep them to yourself.

# BUILDBEST LTD – PROJECT ACTIVITY CHECKLIST

**Project Ref No**.........................................................

**Client**............................. **Project Manager** .................

**Plot No/Location**........................................................

| Activity | Notes |
|---|---|
| 1. **Site**<br>Clear site<br>Drive and paths<br>Landscape<br><br>2. **Shell**<br>Foundations<br>Walls<br>Roof   – carpentry<br>       – tiles/slates<br>Floors  – downstairs<br>       – upstairs<br><br>3. **Finishes**<br>Plastering<br>Painting<br><br>4. **Services**<br>Phone<br>Water<br>Electricity<br>Gas<br>Drains<br>Sewers | |

Fig. 11. A project activity checklist.

## Using checklists

Many companies will run projects as their day-to-day business. For example, a construction company specialising in building bridges will project-manage each bridge, because each site will be unique, even though the bridges might look fairly similar.

*Exercise*
Check that bridge building meets the project criteria, by looking back at the criteria list at the beginning of Chapter 1.

A company running a number of broadly similar projects can draw up a checklist, which will give a good indication of the work required for future projects. For example, a company that builds houses could use a checklist similar to the one illustrated in Figure 11.

The function of the checklist is to act as a prompt, so that the planner does not forget any of the work that needs to be done. The notes section is for details of materials, reference to specifications, or reference to plans.

When drawing up your own project activity checklist, the key points are as follows:

- The checklist can be drawn up after several similar projects have been completed.

- Gather information for the checklist from the project files of previous projects.

- Adapt the checklist as further projects are run.

- Consider adding other sections to the checklist if these will help to act as a memory jogger; for example *Subcontractors chosen*.

## BREAKING DOWN THE WORK DETAILS

In the house building checklist, illustrated in Figure 11, you will notice that it is divided into four main activities: **site, shell, finishes** and **services**. Then each of these activities is divided further; for example, the **shell** into foundations, walls and roof. Then some of these are divided again; for example, the roof requires a carpenter to erect the joists and battens, then another specialist to fit the tiles.

This subdivision of the work is called the **work breakdown structure**. But before we look at the theory, let us see how it works with a case study.

## Moving the major

We will use the private railway company from Chapter 2 for another case study, this time to demonstrate a work breakdown structure.

The director, Major David Mitchell-Jones, has an office in the former waiting room at Hadlow Station. The conditions are far from ideal. It is very cramped, an the company thinks it should be used for its intended purpose, as a waiting room for railway passengers.

The railway extension project is finished, and the new heritage centre in the old engine shed has space for two offices on the first floor. The director is to move into one of these. The existing situation and the planned location of the director's new office is illustrated in Figure 12.

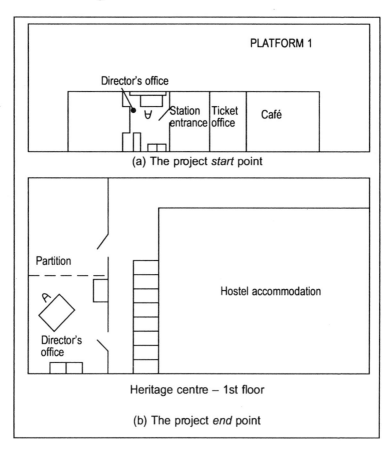

Fig. 12. The office move project.

## Listing the activities

To list all the work that needs to be done for the office move, we use a work breakdown structure.

*Note 1*
The work breakdown structure:

- refers only to work that needs to be done

- does not consider the time it will take to do the work

- does not sort out the order in which the work will be carried out.

The work breakdown structure for the office move is illustrated in Figure 13. The office move divides into two main activity areas: **creating the new office** and **transferring the office contents**. Each of these is then further divided; for example, the **transfer of contents** divides into moving the furniture, and moving the files and personal computer. Below this, there can be a further division of activities to arrive at the final set of boxes. The final set of boxes represents all the work that needs to be done to complete the office move successfully.

*Note 2*
Each branch of the work breakdown structure does not necessarily have the same number of steps down to the final set of boxes.

## Packaging the work

The final set of boxes of a work breakdown structure are called **work packages** or **activities**.
Work packages or activities are:

- self-contained parcels of work, *eg* decorating

- attributable to one person, team of people, or subcontractor, *eg* telephone company.

If we list all the activities for the office move, which are the final set of boxes illustrated in Figure 13, we get an activity list. The activity list for the office above is illustrated in Figure 14.

## Taking the right steps

Now that we have seen how the work for the office move case study

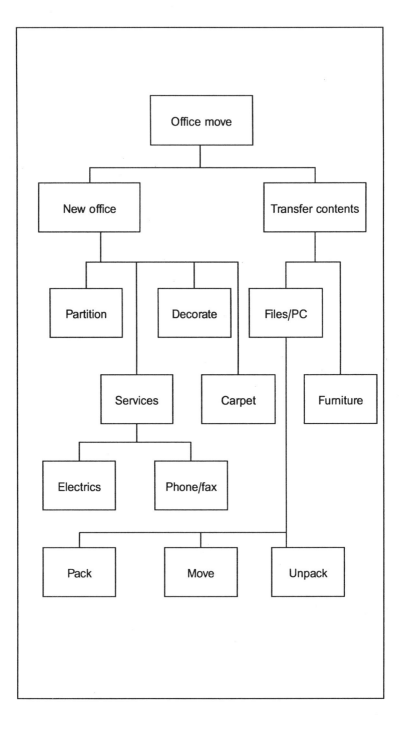

Fig. 13. Office move work breakdown structure.

**The office move – activities**

1. Erect partition to create office space

2. Run cables and fit mains sockets

3. Provide telephone and fax lines

4. Paint and decorate office interior

5. Lay carpet

6. Pack files and personal computer in crates

7. Move crates to new office

8. Move furniture from old to new office

9. Unpack files and personal computer

Fig. 14. Activity list for the office move.

project is identified, using a work breakdown structure, let us review the key steps. These are used for all projects, so the process is very important.

**The work breakdown structure is drawn as a mother and daughter family tree.**

1. Start with the overall objective in the top box, *eg* office move.

2. The next level of boxes will be the major work areas, *eg* create office.

3. The next level of boxes will be the work that needs to be done in each of the major work areas, *eg* provide services.

4. Continue to break down the activities with further levels of boxes, until they can be attributable to one person, a team of people, or a subcontractor, *eg* fit telephone.

5. Use the items in the final set of boxes for the project activity list.

### Taking a different route
It is possible to arrive at the same list of activities for the office move, by using a different arrangement of the work breakdown structure.

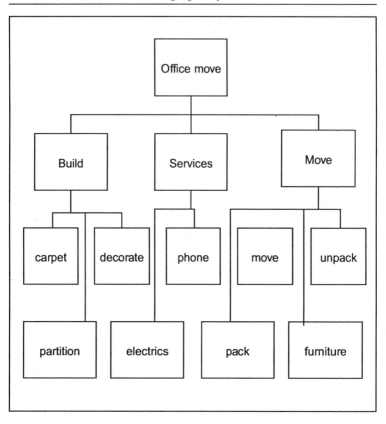

Fig. 15. An alternative work breakdown structure.

If it was decided there were three main activities associated with the office move, rather than just two, then the work breakdown structure would look like the example illustrated in Figure 15. This alternative arrangement still gives a final set of nine boxes identical to those in the work breakdown structure illustrated in Figure 13.

*Important points*
1. The final activity list identified by using a work breakdown structure is always independent of the route taken.

2. Do not waste time disagreeing with other members of the project team over the layout of work breakdown structures, if you have managed to agree over the activities listed in the final set of boxes. How you get there is not important.

*Exercise*

Draw out a work breakdown structure for house building, based on the checklist illustrated in Figure 11. Try to find alternative layouts that give the same activity list.

## ESTIMATING THE COST

The activity list provided by the work breakdown structure is the main source of information for estimating the total cost of the project.

### Costing the Director's move

In the case study to move the Railway Director's office, all the work that needs to be done is recorded in the activity list illustrated in Figure 14. The cost of the project is the cost of each of these activities added together.

The simplest method of adding up these costs is to list the activities on a cost estimate form. The cost estimate form for the case study project is illustrated in Figure 16.

### Allocating suppliers

It is also helpful to record details of who is to do the work, or supply the material. The best place to record this information is to list it alongside the cost figures, on the cost estimate form, as in the case study example illustrated in Figure 16.

*Notes for the case study cost estimate*

1.  The contractors for the partition, phone, painting and carpet will have been selected from quotations from more than one company.

2.  The site electrician, James Jones, is a volunteer worker and is to undertake the electrical work free of charge.

3.  The director will move his own desk and filing cabinets, with the help of volunteers.

4.  Safermoves Ltd are specialists at moving office paperwork and computers. They have special crates to pack the items in. At the other end, they unpack the crates and make sure that everything goes into the right place, and that computers are working.

| COST ESTIMATE | | Project No: HBLR/67/0 | |
|---|---|---|---|

**Estimate for**: Director's office move

**Compiled by**: Laura Smith          Date: 2/3/9X

| No. | Activity | Supplier | Cost |
|---|---|---|---|
| 1 | Erect partition | Buildbest Ltd | £300 |
| 2 | Electrics | James Jones<br>Site electrician<br>Free labour<br>Material cost only | £45 |
| 3 | Phone and fax lines | Holyeside Cable | £250 |
| 4 | Paint and decorate | Hadlow Paints | £375 |
| 5 | Carpet and fitting | Carpetserve | £432 |
| 6<br>7<br>9 | Move files and<br>personal computer<br>to new office | Safermoves Ltd | £150 |
| 8 | Move furniture | D. Mitchell-Jones | nil |
| Total estimated cost: | | | £1,552 |

Fig. 16. Cost estimate form for office move.

52

## Drawing up an estimate form

The cost estimate form, illustrated in Figure 16 for the case study office move, is a simple example. For more complex projects, the cost estimate form may need other columns to provide additional information, for example:

- labour costs
- equipment and material costs
- other expenses such as professional fees
- overhead costs and handling charges
- allowances for inflation, *etc.*

Companies who regularly undertake projects should have their own cost estimate forms prepared as a standard item of company stationery. These are then available for use with any project. To draw up a standard cost estimate form, help from the company accountant or an expert in the company finance department is recommended.

## OBTAINING FINANCIAL AUTHORITY

In the case study, it will cost the railway company £1,552 to move the director to his new office. The Project Manager will need to obtain authority to spend this money, before any work starts.

All projects will require authorisation before work starts. The usual approach is for the Project Manager to prepare a **business case**, to justify spending the money.

The process for obtaining authorisation is illustrated in Figure 17. The preparation of a business case is a key step in this process.

## Documenting the process

It is recommended that companies have a documented procedure for the process of obtaining financial authority for projects. This procedure need not be complicated. For companies involved with straightforward projects, the flowchart illustrated in Figure 17 may be perfectly adequate as a procedure, with very little additional text.

The advantages of documenting the process for obtaining financial authority for projects are as follows:

- Anyone who has been given the job of Project Manager, even for the first time, will know exactly what to do to obtain financial authority.

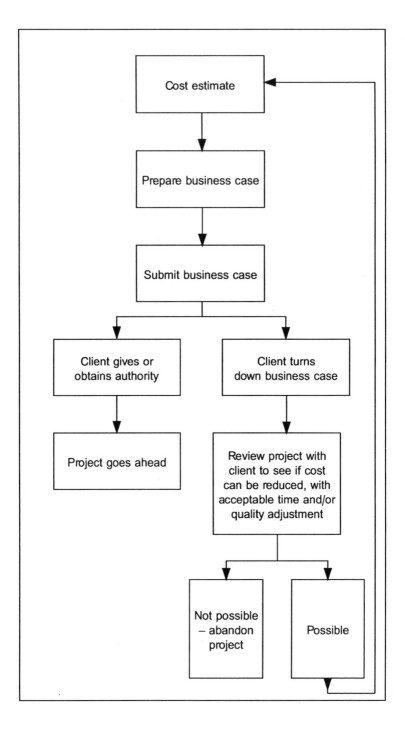

Fig. 17. Process for obtaining financial authority.

54

- Properly costed projects and clearly presented business cases are less likely to get turned down.

- A high success rate for the acceptance of business cases will mean time is not being wasted planning projects that never happen.

*Advice on documenting company procedures*
- Try to use flowcharts as much as possible.

- Avoid detailed descriptions of actions that people are already trained to do, or are likely to be familiar with.

- Concentrate on *what* needs to be done.

*Example*

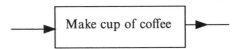

This tells you all you need to know. You should *not* write: 'Carry kettle over to cold tap. Turn on water until kettle is filled to mark, *etc...*'

---

**This advice is valid for all written procedures,
not just for those associated with Project Management.**

---

## Preparing the business case

As part of your company's documented procedures for obtaining financial authority for projects, you should include a standard contents list for business cases. As a minimum, the following main headings are suggested:

1. *Brief description of the project.* To enable a person who is not part of the project to understand what the project objectives are. In many cases it will not be the client who gives authorisation for the work to be done. For example, it could be the company accountant.

2. *Project cost estimate.* Include a list of all the items that make up the total cost. This can be the cost estimate form for simple cases, or a summary if there are a lot of forms. Give an estimate of the accuracy of the figures, *eg* +/- 10 per cent.

3. *Benefits that will result from the project.* Where possible, these should include financial benefits that will offset the project cost. For example, in the office move case study, the station waiting room will become available to passengers. It could also be used during the Christmas period for Santa's Grotto, with the railway running Christmas special trains, adding to the company ticket sales.

4. *Assumptions.* It is necessary for the Project Manager to be honest about how he or she has thought the project through. If assumptions are left out, then the person who has to agree to pay for it might work them out themselves. This would put doubt in his or her mind and weaken the business case. Details of the assumptions should already be available in the client's requirements. An assumption for the office move case study might be: 'It is not going to cost any more to heat the new office compared to the existing one.'

5. *Risks.* This section should cover:

   – risks of not undertaking the project
   – risks if the project does not go to plan.

   Like assumptions, the Project Manager needs to be honest, and demonstrate he or she has dealt with all aspects of the project thoroughly. For the office move case study, examples of each of the above points are:

   – risk of accident and injury to the director if he continues to work in his cramped office
   – risk of new office being too far away from main station buildings, and staff not taking the trouble to consult the director over important issues.

## ESTABLISHING DEPENDENCIES

In the office move case study, so far we have:

1. listed all the work that needs to be done
2. allocated responsibility for doing the work
3. added up how much the work will cost.

*Note*: We will assume a business case is not required – because the client is the director of the railway.

The next step is to sort out which work needs to be done first, and then the order in which the rest of the work must follow. This is important because you would not want the phone company arriving to fit the phone and fax lines, before the partition was put up to create the new office.

## Tabulating dependencies

Each activity of a project will **depend** on one or more of the other activities. In the case study, the phone and fax lines depend on the erection of the partition. To show which activity depends on which other activity, a **dependency table** is drawn up, based on the activity list.

Before a dependency table can be drawn up, the logic of the activities needs to be agreed. This means thinking about the most sensible order for the activities and writing down notes as follows:

*Logic notes for the office move case study*

1. Partition needs to be erected before the telephone and electrics are provided.

2. The telephone and electrics must be finished before the decorators move in.

3. The decorators must finish before the carpet is fitted.

4. Everything in the new office must be ready before starting to pack up in the existing office.

5. The crates must be packed before the furniture can be moved.

6. The furniture must be in the new office before the crates are unpacked.

| No. | Activity | Preceding activity |
|---|---|---|
| 1 | Erect partition to create office | - |
| 2 | Run cables and fit mains sockets | 1 |
| 3 | Provide telephone and fax lines | 1 |
| 4 | Paint and decorate office interior | 2/3 |
| 5 | Lay carpet | 4 |
| 6 | Pack files and PC into crates | 5 |
| 7 | Move crates to new office | 6 |
| 8 | Move furniture from old to new | 6 |
| 9 | Unpack | 7/8 |

Fig. 18. The office move dependency table.

Some of these items are for obvious practical reasons. For example, the reason for Note 3 is the need to avoid dripping paint on the new carpet.

Others may be a personal preference. For example, the reason for Note 4 is the director not wanting to lose the use of his office for longer than necessary.

The dependency table for the office move case study is illustrated in Figure 18. This table is based on the activity list (Figure 14), plus information in the logic notes.

The numbers in the last column of the table are the numbers of the preceding activity on which that activity depends. For example activity 5 – carpet fitting – can't start until the preceding activity 4 – decorate – is finished.

### Creating a network
The best way of showing the order in which project activities need to happen is to use a network diagram. In its simplest form it is a picture of the dependency table. The network diagram of the office move case study is illustrated in Figure 19.

*Notes*
1.  The size of the boxes are always the same. The size does *not* indicate amount of work or time required.

2.  There is no significance in the length of the lines joining the boxes. They are *not* drawn to scale to indicate time.

3.  The importance of the lines between the boxes is that they link dependencies. **Compare the network diagram with the dependency table to see how this work**.

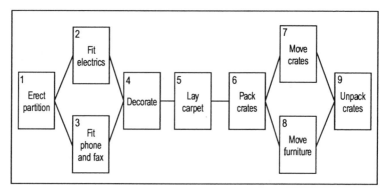

Fig. 19. The office move network diagram.

## Running simple projects

The network diagram describes all the project activities and the order in which they must be done. This will provide sufficient information to run simple projects, like the office move case study. However, for more complex situations, scheduling the activities is essential, so we know exactly when to start each of them. Scheduling is covered in the next chapter.

*Hints to assist you with network diagrams*
1. Each activity should have a number to identify it (first column of the dependency table).

2. Write each activity with its number on a separate self-stick yellow-note.

3. Stick these on a white-board and use dry-wipe pens to draw in the links.

4. Arrive at the solution using a trial and error approach.

## SUMMING UP THE CASE STUDY

The project to move the railway director's office started with the partition being erected. The phone company came to provide the phone and fax lines, but James Jones the site electrician went sick, and he could not come to fit the electrics.

Rather than hold up the decorators, the Project Manager called in a local firm of contractors who completed the work in one day. They charged £250 labour, which had not been included in the original cost estimate.

The director agreed to accept a much cheaper floor covering, to offset this additional cost. Office quality carpet tiles were used, reducing the price by £200. This meant the project overspent by £50, but everything else proceeded without any further snags and the project reached its end point, with the director installed in his new office.

## SUMMARY OF KEY POINTS

### Successful planning
1. Take your time.
2. Avoid too much detail in early stages.
3. Sleep on initial assumptions.
4. Discuss your ideas.

## Checklists
1. For companies running projects as their day-to-day business.
2. Act as prompts for work that needs to be done.
3. Draw up checklist using information from previous projects.
4. Adapt as experience is gained while using the checklist.

## The work breakdown structure
1. Identifies all the work that needs to be done.
2. Drawn as a mother/daughter family tree.
3. Lowest set of boxes represent self-contained work items, attributable to one person, a team, or a subcontractor.
4. Activity list is taken from lowest set of boxes.
5. Activity list is independent of route taken to draw out the work breakdown structure.

## Costing the project
1. Draw up a cost estimate form.
2. Transfer details from activity list.
3. Allocate suppliers.
4. Cost each activity.
5. Add up costs to give total.

## Obtaining financial authority
1. Have a documented procedure and standard business case contents for your company.
2. Submit business case in accordance with company procedures.
3. Reduce cost by adjusting quality and time objectives, if business case is not accepted.
4. Resubmit reviewed business case.

## Dependencies
1. Each activity must have an identity number.
2. Discuss and record logic of project activities.
3. Draw up a dependency table, based on activity list and logic.
4. Draw a network diagram to illustrate dependencies and order of activities.

## CASE STUDIES

### I spy a clever checklist
The Spyder Eye Security Company specialises in close circuit television installations (CCTV). It provides a range of cameras and

methods of fixing, and several control room options.

Each installation is unique, and Project Management techniques are used to plan and deliver exactly what the customer wants.

The company sales personnel use a detailed checklist when discussing requirements with customers. This checklist has evolved out of many years of experience with CCTV projects. The planning office then uses the information from the completed checklist as the basis for the work breakdown structure. This information is fed into a personal computer, which has been programmed to carry out a cost estimate.

Spyder Eye Security has a good reputation, which makes it a natural choice for customers. It is an efficient and professional company, largely due to its highly effective Project Management techniques.

## St Mary's bells saved by Project Management

When Stephen, the new vicar of St Mary's, arrives in Hadlow, he finds the church in a very poor state of repair. Things are so bad that the congregation has had to move into the church hall for their Sunday services.

Stephen goes to the Bishop to see if funds are available to restore the church. The Bishop is sympathetic, and he suggests if Stephen can come up with an accurate cost estimate, then the Diocese may be prepared to fund part of it.

Laura, who project-managed the Hadlow Branch Line Railway extension, is a member of St Mary's congregation, and she offers to help. A small project team is formed, with the project end point planned as the ringing of the bells for the first service back in the church.

The project team produces a work breakdown structure of all the work that needs to be done. From this they undertake a feasibility cost estimate, by asking local companies to submit estimates for each of the activities.

A business case is submitted to the Bishop, and agreement is reached that the Diocese will fund 80 per cent of the work, with the parish raising the rest by staging local fund-raising events.

These fund-raising events, such as a sponsored pram push and attic sales, are included as project activities and they appear as boxes in the network diagram.

The project is managed by using the network diagram as the main guide, and two years after starting, St Mary's reopens to the sound of its own bells.

## Simon says he's in control

The Hoyle Regional Health Authority Ambulance Service wants to improve its efficiency, to give sharper response times and reduce running costs.

The current operations are manually controlled. The Ambulance Service Director thinks an up-to-date computer controlled system is the answer. But similar controls in other health authorities have had a lot of teething troubles, leading to patients' lives being put at risk, and the authorities getting a bad press.

Simon is a consultant brought in from a long established Project Management company. He will project-manage the changeover to the new control system, supported by a project team drawn from the authority's own staff.

After the work breakdown structure has been completed, considerable care and attention is given to the logic of the project activities. This is very important because the authority needs to be certain that the dependencies are accurately defined. One of the key logic items, and a dependency for all other project activities, is that the computer system is observed to be working effectively in a similar situation with another health authority.

As the project nears completion, and the new control room is about to go live, nothing that needed to be done has been omitted or bypassed. The subsequent changeover takes place without any snags and the new control room goes on to provide the expected quality of service with significantly reduced running costs.

## DISCUSSION POINTS

1.  The cost estimate for the office move case study was a feasibility estimate. Because the electrical work had to be undertaken by a contractor, instead of being free of charge as was originally planned, the project cost £50 more than expected. Calculate this as a percentage of the original estimate, to verify that it falls within the +/- 10 per cent accuracy rule. If the cost of the carpet had not been reduced, would the cost estimate still have been within these limits?

2.  Companies are advised to document their procedures for the submission of business cases. Who do you think should write the procedures? What are the advantages and disadvantages of employing specialists as procedure writers?

3. In the office move case study, assume it takes one day to pack the crates, and one day to lay the carpet in the new office. If the director agreed, the crates could be packed on the same day as the carpet was being fitted. Amend the dependency table accordingly, and redraw the network diagram to show this new arrangement. *Hint*: the 'lay carpet' and 'pack crates' activities in the network diagram will be in parallel.

# 4
# Finding Critical Paths

## ANALYSING THE NETWORK

The network diagram, as in the example illustrated in Figure 19, shows the order in which each activity of a project should be done. It also clarifies which activities need to be finished before subsequent activities can start. In this chapter we will look at how **time** is included, to give a detailed schedule for the project.

### Choosing the most appropriate picture
For reasons that will be explained later, scheduling project activities comes under the general heading of Critical Path Analysis (CPA).

One method of picturing a network that includes time is called an arrow diagram. However, in this book we will carry out CPA based on the network diagram introduced in the previous chapter.

### Coping with CPA
Working with CPA networks is quite tricky, and the whole CPA process can be a little frustrating. Just when you think you have got it right, you may spot another error and have to try again. And the larger the network, the more messy it seems to get. Remember, however, that CPA is:

- tricky even for people who are familiar with the technique

- only simple addition and subtraction, with no complicated mathematics

- best approached using trial and error.

A case study will be used to demonstrate how to do CPA. But before that let us look at how the activity box is expanded to include additional time information.

## Expanding the activity box

The standard CPA network activity box is illustrated in Figure 20. The shape of this box is identical with those in the network diagram used in the last chapter, but its inside is divided up as follows:

- a top row of three pigeon holes
- an open rectangle across the middle
- a bottom row of three pigeon holes.

The activity boxes in the network diagram in the last chapter already include the activity number and the activity description. (Look back at the network diagram illustrated in Figure 19.) This is the same information that will appear in the middle of the CPA activity box.

The top row and bottom row of pigeon holes are used for **time** information. The different times that go into each pigeon hole are illustrated in the upper diagram of Figure 20. All CPA activity boxes are the same, no matter where they are in the CPA network.

| Earliest start | Duration | Earliest finish |
|---|---|---|
| Activity number Activity description | | |
| Latest start | Total float | Latest finish |

|  |  |  |
|---|---|---|
|  | | |
|  |  |  |

Fig. 20. The standard activity box for CPA.

The case study will make clear what each item means in practice, but before that, here are the formal definitions. You may wish to refer to these while undertaking CPA.

*Earliest start*
The earliest date on which the activity can start.

*Duration*
How long the activity will take.

*Earliest finish*
The earliest date the activity will be finished.

*Latest start*
The latest date the activity can start, without affecting the remainder of the project.

*Total float*
The amount of time the activity can shift, without affecting the project.

*Latest finish*
The latest time the activity can finish without affecting the project.

*Note*: All times are in days.

*Example:*
Earliest start: day 4.
Duration:     3 days.

*Hint*
Photocopy lots of empty CPA activity boxes (use the lower blank box in Figure 20). The boxes can be stuck on a white-board with Blu-tack. Join them up, to make the CPA network, with a dry marker pen. Activity details can then be written in, as the analysis progresses. This arrangement will give you the flexibility for a trial and error approach.

## UNRAVELLING THE MYSTERIES OF CPA

The case study that follows demonstrates how to do Critical Path Analysis (CPA).

## Putting on an exhibition

Hoyle District Council is to put on a Trades Exhibition in Hadlow Civic Hall. It will last for five days, from Monday to Friday, and cater for local companies to display their products and services.

To simplify the project for the purposes of the case study, the following points apply:

1. The project end point will be when the exhibition opens.

2. All the applications from exhibitors have been received and accepted. There is space available for all of them.

3. Advertising, ticket printing, car parking, *etc* have been excluded from the case study.

## Clarifying the dependencies

To arrive at the dependency table for the exhibition project, the Project Manager and the team will have carried out a work breakdown structure. There would also have been a discussion about the order and logic of the activities.

The activities for the case study are as follows:

1. *Start*
   *Duration*: 0 days     *Depends on*: none
   This is a **dummy activity** used to link two branches at the beginning of the network. Refer to the illustration in Figure 22 (page 70) to see how activity no. 1. is used.

2. *Allocation*
   *Duration*: 3 days     *Depends on*: 1
   This activity is to sort out which company gets which exhibition stand.

3. *Open hall*
   *Duration*: 1 day     *Depends on*: 1
   The Civic Hall is to be cleared of tables and chairs used by the local WI, and made ready to receive the exhibition stands.

4. *Publish plan*
   *Duration*: 2 days     *Depends on*: 2
   A plan of the hall is drawn up to show the location of the stands and the company names.

| No. | Activity | Preceding activity | Duration |
|---|---|---|---|
| 1 | Start | - | - |
| 2 | Allocate stands | 1 | 3 days |
| 3 | Open hall | 1 | 1 day |
| 4 | Publish layout plan | 2 | 2 days |
| 5 | Deliver stands | 3 | 2 days |
| 6 | Train stewards | 4 | 1 day |
| 7 | Erect stands | 4/5 | 2 days |
| 8 | Set up exhibition | 6/7 | 3 days |
| 9 | Train staff | 7 | 1 day |
| 10 | Open exhibition | 8/9 | – |

| Week | 1 | | | | | 2 | | | | | 3 | | | |
|---|---|---|---|---|---|---|---|---|---|---|---|---|---|---|
| Day | 1 | 2 | 3 | 4 | 5 | 6 | 7 | 8 | 9 | 10 | 11 | | | |

Fig. 21. Exhibition dependency table and calendar.

5. *Deliver stands*
   *Duration*: 2 days      *Depends on*: 3
   Exhibition stands will be supplied by a subcontractor. It takes them one day to load the lorry at their warehouse, then another day to transport and unload them.

6. *Train stewards*
   *Duration*: 1 day      *Depends on*: 4
   The stewards will direct the exhibitors to their stands and generally assist them while they set up their displays. Training is in the classroom and based on the published layout plan.

7. *Erect stands*
   *Duration*: 2 days      *Depends on*: 4 and 5
   The subcontractors will set up the exhibition stands in accordance with the published layout plan.

8. *Set up*
   *Duration*: 3 days      *Depends on*: 6 and 7
   The exhibitors set up their own displays on the stands provided.

9. *Train staff*
   *Duration*: 1 day      *Depends on*: 7
   The staff who will be on hand during the exhibition need to be familiar with the hall when it is filled with the erected stands. This is for safety reasons.

10. *Open exhibition*
    *Duration*: 0 days      *Depends on*: 8 and 9
    Another **dummy activity** to indicate the project end point.

## Understanding the calendar

The dependency table for the exhibition case study is illustrated in Figure 21. Also included with the dependency table is a simple calendar to help clarify start and finish times.

The calendar for the exhibition case study CPA works as follows:

• A five-day working week has been used.

• The exhibition case study will open at the beginning of week 3, that is on day 11. Everything must be ready on the Friday before, that is day 10.

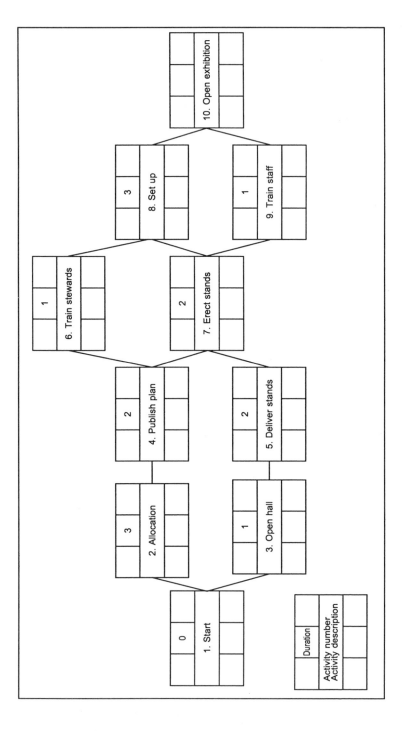

Fig. 22. CPA network – activities and durations.

- An activity with a duration of 1 day starts and finishes on the same day. For example, an activity starting on day 2, with a duration of 1 day, will use up the whole of day 2, and finish on day 2.

- The activity which follows on from the above activity will start on day 3. If this lasts three days, then it will finish on day 5.

*Hint*: count the days on your fingers.

## PLOTTING THE PATHS

The CPA network is drawn from the dependency table in exactly the same way as the network diagram in the last chapter.

### Adding description and duration
The CPA network for the exhibition case study is illustrated in Figure 22. For this first step the network has been drawn using the information from the dependency table, to show:

- which activity depends on which other activities
- the activity numbers and descriptions
- the duration of each activity (in days).

### Passing forward
To calculate the earliest start and earliest finish times, which are the two other pigeon holes on the top row of the activity boxes, a **forward pass** is made. This means moving from left to right through each branch of the network. For the exhibition case study, the result is illustrated in Figure 23.

Starting with the following path through the network: $1 \rightarrow 2 \rightarrow 4 \rightarrow 7 \rightarrow 8 \rightarrow 10$.

*Activity 2*    Allocating the exhibition stands starts on day 1. It takes 3 days. Earliest finish is day 3.

*Activity 4*    Publishing the plans can be started on day 4, because activity 2 was finished at the end of day 3. Activity 4 takes 2 days. Earliest finish is day 5.

*Activity 7*    Earliest start is day 6. It takes 2 days. Earliest finish is day 7.

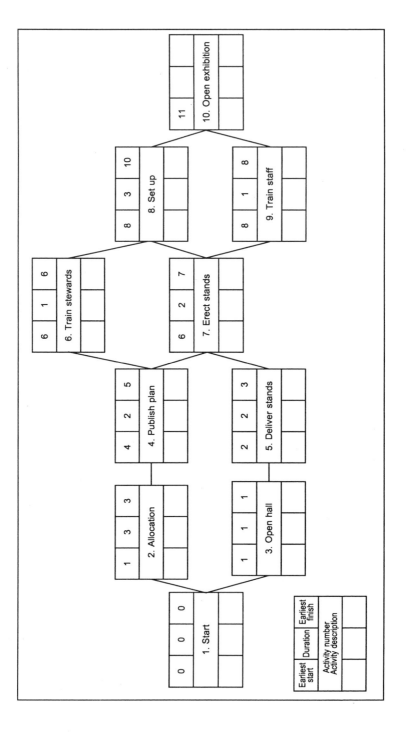

Fig. 23. CPA network – the forward pass.

*Activity 8*     Earliest start is day 8. It takes 3 days. Earliest finish is day 10.

*Activity 10*    Earliest start is day 11. The exhibition opens on day 11.

The next path ($1 \rightarrow 3 \rightarrow 5 \rightarrow 7 \rightarrow 9 \rightarrow 10$) can now be completed with another forward pass. Where activity 5 feeds into activity 7, you will end up with a different answer for the earliest start time for activity 7, compared to that from the first forward pass. But the stands can't be erected until the plan is published, so activity 7 must take the later of the two possible earliest start dates.

Depending on which route through the network you choose to do first, you will usually find you have to alter some of the times as you cover other paths.

*Exercise*
Try path $1 \rightarrow 2 \rightarrow 4 \rightarrow 6 \rightarrow 8 \rightarrow 10$ for yourself to check the details in the activity 6 box.

## Passing backwards
To calculate the latest start and latest finish times, which are in the lower row of pigeon holes, a backward pass is made through the network. For the exhibition case study, the result is illustrated in Figure 24.

The starting point for a backward pass is the final activity. In the case study this is activity no. 8. Activity 8 is the last item of work to be done – the exhibitors setting up their displays. Activity 8 finishes on day 10.

*Activity 8*     The earliest finish is day 10. Latest finish is also day 10. (This is always the case for the final activity.) The latest start, with a duration of 3 days, must be day 8.

*Activity 9*     This activity can finish on day 8. Day 8 is its earliest finish. It can also finish as late as day 10. So its latest finish is day 10. Latest start, with a duration of 1 day, is day 10. What this means is that we can delay the start of activity 9, training the staff, until day 10, without it affecting the project.

*Activity 7*     The latest start for the following activity, activity 8, is day 8. So the latest finish for activity 7 will be the

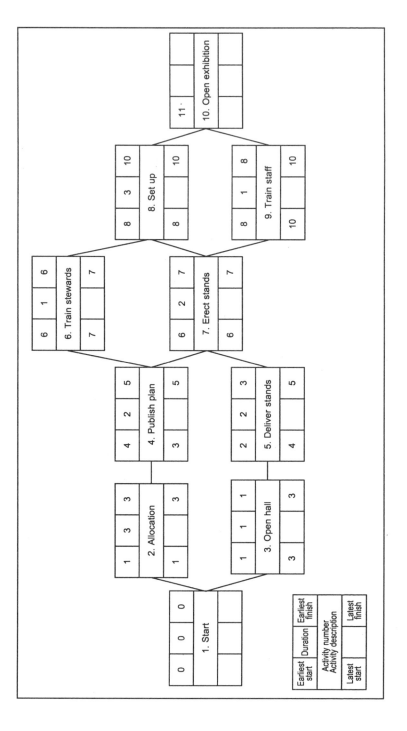

Fig. 24. CPA network – the backward pass.

74

previous day, day 7. With a duration of 2 days, this means the latest start is day 6.

*Note*: Activity 9 does not affect the latest finish of activity 7, because it can wait until day 10 before it has to start.

This process is continued back through the network, to complete the latest finish and start dates for each of the activities. Where the network splits into two parallel branches, the latest finish dates are always the same. For example, passing backwards from activity 8 to activities 6 and 7.

*Hints*
1. For a backward pass remember to work through the bottom set of pigeon holes only.
2. All the key steps of how to make forward and backward passes are summarised later in this chapter, which will help to make these processes much clearer.

## Identifying the critical path
The remaining pigeon hole in the activity boxes is the one in the middle of the bottom row: **total float**. This is now many days the activity can be delayed, without it affecting the project.

The total float is calculated for each activity using:

$$\text{latest finish} - \text{earliest finish}$$

For activity 6:

$$\text{total float} = 7 - 6 = 1 \text{ day}$$

For the exhibition case study, the complete CPA network is illustrated in Figure 25. The heavy line indicates the path through the network, via activities with a **zero total float**. This is the **critical path**.

Features of the critical path are as follows:

• All of the activities on the critical path must start and finish on time, if the project is to meet its **time** objectives.

• The total project duration is the sum of the activity duration, added up along the critical path.

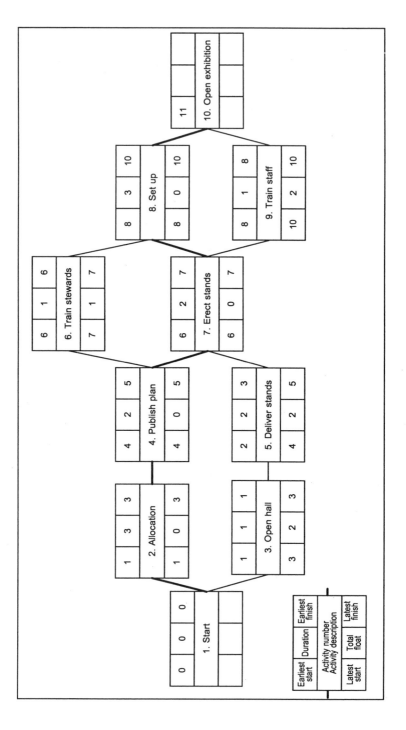

Fig. 25. CPA network – total float and critical path.

## SUMMING UP CRITICAL PATH ANALYSIS (CPA)

CPA is tricky, but straightforward with a little practice. The best way to learn how to do it is to try some examples for yourself.

### Practising CPA
The following exercise is suggested to help you with CPA.

1. Choose some of the case studies given at the end of Chapters 1, 2 and 3, or from within the main text of these chapters.

2. Think up a suitable work breakdown structure, if one is not included as part of the case study details.

3. Think about the logic of the activities and draw up a dependency table. Add durations to each activity. The durations need not be accurate for the purposes of this exercise.

4. Draw the CPA network and calculate all the times. Mark the critical path.

5. Give the same data to a friend or colleague to see if they come up with the same results. Compare answers and learn from your mistakes.

### Listing the key steps
Here is a list of the key steps for CPA. This can be used as a prompt list for the exercise above, and for real CPA situations.

| Key steps | Notes |
|---|---|
| 1. *Draw the network* | |
| • Draw the network using standard activity boxes. | |
| • Enter the activity number, description and duration (D). | |
| 2. *Make a forward pass* | |
| • Start with first activity, enter earliest start (ES) as day 1. | |
| • Calculate earliest finish (EF). | $EF = ES + D - 1$ |
| • Enter ES for subsequent activity. | $ES = EF$ (previous activity) $+ 1$ |

- Continue process to end of network.

- Repeat for other branches          (Adjust times as necessary)

3. *Make a backward pass*
- Use the EF in the final activity          Final activity always
  for the latest finish (LF).                       has LF = EF

- Calculate latest start (LS).          $LS = LF - D + 1$

- Enter LF for previous activity.          $LF + LS$ (subsequent activity) $- 1$

- Continue process for rest of network.

- Repeat for other branches.

4. *Identify the critical path*
- For each activity calculate          $TF = LF - EF$
  total float (TF).

- Mark critical path between
  activity boxes with zero float.

## CHARTING PROJECT ACTIVITIES

The CPA network is drawn for the following reasons:

- to calculate activity start and finish times
- to calculate total project time
- to identify the critical path.

CPA is a method the Project Manager and his or her team are intimately involved in. However, outsiders, for example senior managers and subcontractors, will find it easier to understand the project by looking at charts derived from the CPA network.

### Planning with a Gantt chart

The bar chart used in Project Management is called a Gantt chart. This is named after an American engineer Henry Gantt. The Gantt chart for the exhibition case study is illustrated in Figure 26.

   Gantt chart key points are as follows:

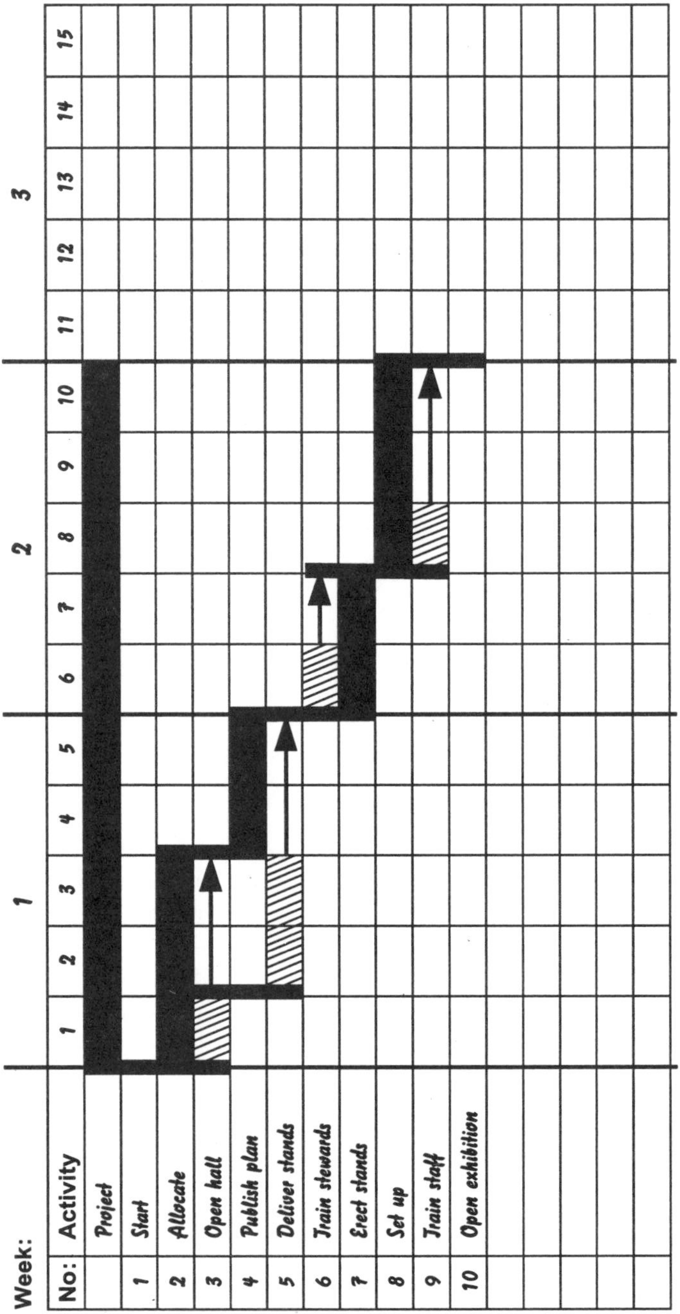

Fig. 26. Gantt chart for the exhibition.

- Critical activities, that is those along the critical path, are shown as solid bars.

- Non-critical activities, that is those with a float, are shown as cross-hatched.

- The overall project time is shown as a single bar across the top.

- The links between the activities, that is the lines joining the boxes on the CPA network, are shown as bold vertical lines.

- Floats are indicated by arrows.

## Using Gantt charts

The Gantt chart is a simple but very useful Project Management tool.

The Gantt chart has the following **advantages**:

- An easy to interpret picture of the project.

- A summary of the project that can usually be on just one page.

- Shows critical activities and those that can be allowed to start later.

- Can be used to monitor progress by marking off activities as they are completed.

The style of Gantt chart for the exhibition case study, drawn by hand on a standard form, does have a couple of **disadvantages**:

- Vertical linking of activities gets difficult with complex projects.

- The chart needs to be redrawn each time there is a delay or other change.

Both of these problems can be adequately addressed when using a computer software package. This is explained in Chapter 6.

## Drawing your own Gantt charts

If you are likely to be involved in a number of projects, then it's a good idea to prepare a form for drawing Gantt charts. This can be done using a personal computer, then photocopying to provide plenty of blanks.

Base the design on the Gantt chart illustrated in Figure 26. The following notes offer further guidance:

1.  Expand the form if necessary, adding more weeks and/or activity lines.

2.  Add a heading to include project name, title, and other details.

3.  Make your weeks six days if work is done on Saturdays. Seven if Sundays are included.

4.  The *week* boxes across the top can be: *Week commencing...  Week 1, 2, 3, etc*, or whatever suits your company.

## OPTIMISING RESOURCES

With a Gantt chart, you can see at a glance when all the resources for the project are required. Resources will include:

- people and labour
- materials
- renting and hiring.

### Minimising expenditure

In the exhibition case study, the Gantt chart illustrated in Figure 26, indicates that the hall is to be opened on day 1. But the hall does not have to be opened until day 3, because there is a 2-day total float for this activity. By opening the hall on day 3, the rent bill would be reduced by 2 days.

### Avoiding overlaps

The Gantt chart also displays the relationship between the activities. It shows those that follow on from another activity. And it shows those that overlap and run in parallel.

Parallel activities can be a problem, particularly in projects with a large number of activities. Let's look at an example:

*Factory unit project*
*Activity 34* Brickwork for security lodge
*Activity 67* Brickwork for perimeter wall

Assume that Gantt chart for this project indicates that:

- part of these two activities run in parallel
- there is an overlap of 3 days with only 1 day float for each activity
- there is only one team of bricklayers available.

Clearly the bricklayers can't be in two places at the same time.

*The solution is to:*

1. Redraw the CPA network, to put a **link** in between the two activities, to make one activity dependent on the other.

2. Revise the Gantt chart to match the change in the CPA network.

### Waiting for the paint to dry

Sometimes it is necessary to add further activities to impose delays, to allow for things like:

– paint to dry
– concrete to set
– turf to bed in.

These activities do not themselves use up any resources, but the delay can cause additional expenditure; for example, paying bricklayers to wait until foundations have set, before they can start constructing the walls of a building.

Adding further activities to indicate delays will mean the workforce arrives at the right time to start their work.

## SUMMING UP PROJECT PLANNING

The overall planning process is illustrated in Figure 27. This process includes a route back to the CPA network for any adjustments that have to be made as a result of optimising resources.

Companies wishing to document their project planning procedure can use this flowchart as the basic outline. Anyone called upon to run, or be involved in, project work will follow the standard company procedure.

The advantages of having a company procedure for Project Management are that it:

1. ensures a consistent approach by all departments

2. makes it more likely that projects will meet objectives

3. provides a useful guide for those unfamiliar with Project Management techniques.

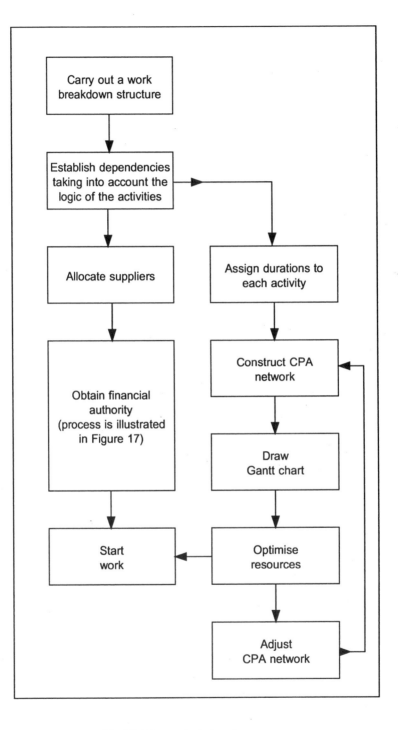

Fig. 27. The project planning process.

## EXHIBITING SUCCESS

For the exhibition case study, the Gantt chart was copied and issued to everyone involved in the project, so they could see how they fitted into the overall plan.

The hall was opened on day 1 because the subcontractors asked if they could deliver the stands on day 2. The stands were already at another site so this would save returning them to the warehouse. The cost of the delivery and erection of the stands was reduced by 10 per cent, which offset the additional days the hall was hired for.

The Hoyle District Council Trades Exhibition opened on time, thanks to effective Project Management.

## SUMMARY OF KEY POINTS

### Critical Path Analysis
1. Usually abbreviated to CPA.
2. Best approach is by trial and error.
3. The standard CPA network activity box displays the activity description and time information.

### Carrying out CPA
1. Give each activity a duration, as part of the dependency table.
2. Draw the CPA network using standard activity boxes.
3. Add in descriptions and durations.
4. Make a forward pass to calculate earliest starts and finishes.
5. Make a backward pass to calculate latest starts and finishes.
6. Calculate total floats and identify critical path.
7. Practise the technique to become familiar with it.

### The Gantt chart
1. A bar chart based on information in the CPA network.
2. Shows critical path, links between activities, non-critical activities and floats.

### Resources
1. Optimise resources to reduce costs and avoid overlapping activities.
2. Adjust CPA network to match optimised resources.
3. Redraw Gantt chart if necessary.

## Project planning
Document the process as part of company procedures.

## CASE STUDIES

### Varley Cars take to the road
Edward Varley, a former London cab driver, has moved from the City to Hadlow, where he intends to set up his own private hire taxi company.

With a little help from his brother, who works for a building firm, Edward project-manages the creation of his new taxi company. The activities are identified as: open an office, install a telephone system, install a radio base station, take on owner-drivers, fit radios in the cars, select reception staff, advertise Varley Cars, draw up rotas.

A CPA network is constructed, then a Gantt chart. The Gantt chart shows that the telephone fitter would be working in the small office at the same time as the installer fitting the radio base station. The CPA network and the Gantt chart were amended to avoid this overlap.

With everything taken care of by effective Project Management, Varley Cars is on the road at the planned start date and operating at full strength.

### Heralding the end of the *Gazette*
The *Hadlow Gazette*, a local weekly newspaper, is to cease publication after sixty years. Richard, the owner, has decided to retire and sell the *Gazette* to the much larger *Ness Herald*.

He thinks that the best way to close the *Gazette* down, with minimal stress and disruption to the employees, is to manage the closure as a project. The activities include the transfer of some of the work and staff to the *Herald* office, and the shutdown of the *Gazette* office and production facilities.

The CPA network has a critical path of three months. The *Herald* management were expecting a more rapid closure, but when they are shown a copy of the Gantt chart, they accept that the project has more to it than they first realised.

The plans are accepted and the closure goes ahead, keeping to the specified time-scales.

### Vikki project-manages her own success
Vikki has recently graduated with a maths degree from Hoyle University. She has remained in the town, close to the university,

while she tries to find employment.

Hoyle is a new university, which is growing fast, and the small town of Hoyle can't provide sufficient student accommodation. Unable to find a suitable job, Vikki sets up her own company: Hoyle Student Housing. Her intention is to buy run-down houses, and convert these into student flats.

Although Vikki knows little about building work, by using Project Management skills she is able to plan all the work that needs to be done. Subcontractors then submit tenders for the work, and say how long the work will take. This information is then used to produce detailed plans in the form of CPA networks and Gantt charts.

Starting with just one house, bought with a bank loan, within two years Vikki is running a highly successful company.

## DISCUSSION POINTS

1.  In the exhibition case study, the Gantt chart shows the delivery of stands starting immediately after the hall is open. What changes to the chart result from the subcontractor being able to bring the stands directly from their previous location?

2.  In the exhibition case study, how would you establish the start date for the project?

3.  When you use the case studies from previous chapters to practise CPA, will it be more appropriate to count in weeks or months, rather than days, for some of them?

# 5
# Monitoring the Work

## KEEPING THE PROJECT UNDER CONTROL

Work begins when the project moves from the specify stage into the produce stage. In this chapter, we will see how the progress of the work is monitored and controlled. This is important because we need to ensure the time, cost and quality objectives agreed with the client are delivered.

### Monitoring and controlling

The Project Manager is responsible for delivering the project objectives. While the work is going on, he or she must:

**Monitor** the work  – measure its progress

**Control** the work  – take action to ensure it stays on track.

These two actions are linked together as a continuous process. The monitor/control process is illustrated as a flowchart in Figure 28.

### Keeping the project on track

The monitor and control process works as follows (refer to the flowchart, illustrated in Figure 28, as each step is explained):

*Measure progress*
- When did each activity start and finish, and/or what percentage has been completed?

- How much has been spent so far?

- What is the quality of workmanship?

*Compare results*
- Where should each activity be up to according to Gantt chart?

- What was the estimated cost of the project at this point?

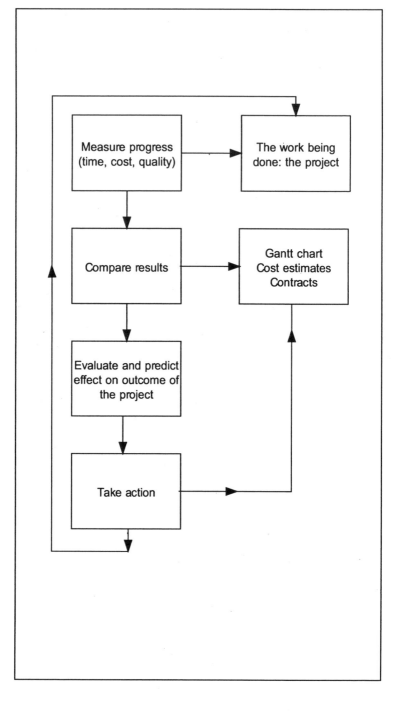

Fig. 28. The project monitor and control process.

- What was agreed in contracts and/or at project team meetings?

*Evaluate and predict*
- Assess the effect of differences on the overall project.

- Place emphasis on areas which have the most effect – usually activities on the critical path.

*Take action*
- Take appropriate action to bring project back on track.

- Update plans.

## MEASURING PROGRESS

To measure the progress of a project, a progress reporting process must be in place as soon as the work starts. In the flowchart illustrated in Figure 28, progress reporting is represented by the link between the measure and work boxes.

### Reporting progress
Referring back to the case study project team meeting agenda, illustrated in Figure 9, item 4 is: 'Progress reports from individual team members.'

Now have a look at the typical project file contents, illustrated in Figure 10. Item 7 is 'monitoring and control'.

---

**The Project Manager must include a mechanism for progress reporting as part of his or her plans.**

---

There are a number of different options available for progress reporting, which we will now look at.

### Going walkabout
One of the essential qualities of a Project Manager is that they are a person who likes to see what is going on for themselves. When they are visiting the work being done, they listen and take note of what is being said by the people doing the work. These items feature in the score card for selection of Project Managers, illustrated in Figure 4.

A person who never leaves their desk to view the work, or who always sees things through rose-tinted spectacles, will not be able to monitor and control a project effectively.

## Gathering information

Regular reports are an effective process for gathering the information required in order to monitor a project. The frequency of reporting will depend on the project duration. A rough rule of thumb is to expect around ten reports between the project start and end. For convenience, the frequency of reports should be monthly, weekly or daily (as appropriate). (See Figure 29.)

| Project duration | Reporting frequency | Typical reporting methods |
|---|---|---|
| 12 months | Monthly | Detailed report or standard report form – via post, fax or e-mail. Monthly meeting. |
| 2 months | Weekly | Standard report form – via fax or e-mail. Phone call. Weekly meeting. |
| 2 weeks | Daily | Phone call. Project Manager meets team members and subcontractors on site each day. |

Fig. 29. Project reporting frequencies and methods.

The method of reporting will vary according to the duration of the project. However, it is the Project Manager's responsibility to specify the reporting method. Examples of reporting frequency and methods are illustrated in Figure 29.

A standard form that can be used by project team members to make monthly reports is illustrated in Figure 30. One form is required for each activity. All the details, down as far as *progress*, but not including the *month* at the top, can be filled in by the Project Manager before giving the forms to the team members. The project team members then photocopy the forms, to make their reports on.

The *earliest start* and *finish* are from the CPA network activity box or the Gantt chart – converted into calendar dates.

End of_____

## MONTHLY PROGRESS REPORT

Project title:_____ No.:_____

From_____ (name/dept)

ACTIVITY:_____ No.:_____

Earliest start date:_____

Earliest finish date:_____

Estimated cost/resources required:_____

_____

**Progress**

% completed_____ Estimated finish date:_____

Spend so far/resources used:_____

Estimated spend/resources used on completion of activity:_____

_____

Workmanship meeting requirements as per contract or specification:

_____

_____

**Impact of any variation from plans**

_____

_____

Signed_____ Date_____

Fax report to Project Manager on last working day each month.
FAX 01237 XXXXXXXXX

Fig. 30. Example form for monthly progress reporting.

### Collating reports

The Project Manager will collate the information from the reports he or she receives, and produce an overall project report – if this is required for:

- the client

- other project managers who have related projects

- a programme controller – where a number of company projects are being co-ordinated as part of an overall programme.

## TAKING APPROPRIATE ACTION

The Project Manager considers all the information from reports and decides if any action is required.

It is important that individual members of the project team do not take action on their own, even if they can see that things are getting behind, or too much is being spent.

Only the Project Manager has an overall view of the project. An overspend in one area may be offset by an underspend in another.

### Deciding on the action

Action to ensure project objectives are met fall into the three main areas of: time, cost and quality.

*Time-scales*

When time-scales are threatened, the following action is available:

- Check assumptions made during planning.
- Use overtime.
- Move resources around.
- Change skill level of workforce.
- Minimise travelling time.
- Try a different method of working.
- Reorganise order of tasks.

*Spend/resources*

If a project is using up more resources, or is costing more than estimated, the following action is available:

- Increase efficiency of work.
- Improve control of purchasing.

- Seek alternative suppliers.
- Change specifications.

*Quality*
If the project appears to be heading towards failing to meet its quality objectives, the Project Manager can do the following:

- Review testing and acceptance criteria.

- Review specifications/contracts with subcontractors to ensure they are conforming to requirements.

- Introduce spot checks and inspections while work is going on.

## Authorising change
If the action required to get the project back on track means making a significant change, authority may be required from the client or senior management. The change process is detailed later in this chapter.

## KEEPING THE WORK ON TRACK

Let's look at a case study to see how project monitoring and control works in practice.

## Inheriting an opportunity
Bruce is working in Australia as a Project Manager for a Brisbane construction company, when he inherits his uncle's farm in England. He gives up his job and flies back to England.

Woods Farm turns out to be a bit of a disappointment. It is not a working farm. It has only one small field for ponies. But there is a house and some old farm buildings, a dozen ponies and plenty of chickens which scratch a living from the muddy farmyard.

A near neighbour, a local councillor, suggests that Bruce should consider setting up a children's farm. This would cater for visitors at weekends, school parties, and provide jobs for the local young unemployed.

## Planning for success
Bruce draws up plans and obtains planning permission for the children's farm. The proposal is illustrated in Figure 31, and the Gantt chart for the activities is illustrated in Figure 32. Details of the activities are as follows:

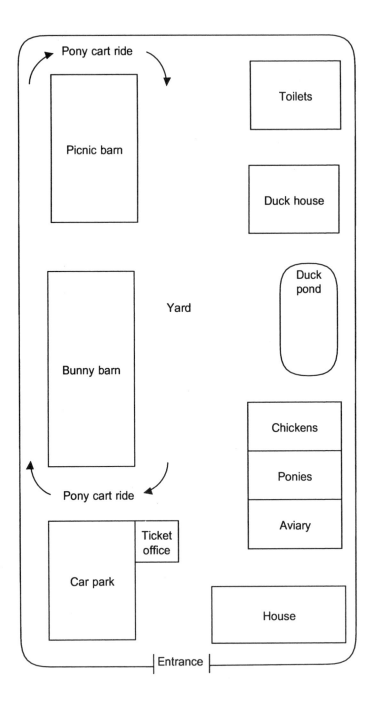

Fig. 31. The children's farm case study.

1.  *Yard and paths.* Laying concrete surface over farmyard area and pathways. Also around pony cart ride. It will take 3 days to lay concrete then another 4 days to harden. Hardening time includes a Saturday and Sunday.

2.  *Bunny barn.* Existing timber framed barn is to be home for a large collection of rabbits and other furry animals. Supplier of animals, cages and runs will be the local pet specialist – Hoyle Pet Stores Ltd.

3.  *Lights.* The Bunny Barn is to be fitted with electric lighting. Bruce will do this work himself.

4.  *Duck pond.* A pond is to be excavated, lined and filled with water. Work by Ness Park Aquatics.

5.  *Duck house.* A poultry shed is to be erected next to the duck pond, to provide secure overnight accommodation for the ducks.

6.  *Ticket office.* A standard summer house will be used at the entrance for the ticket sales office. To be supplied by Hoyle Sheds and Conservatories. Once the ticket office is in place, large items such as the toilets will not be able to get past.

7.  *Car park.* To be surfaced with gravel supplied and spread by the local building company, Buildbest Ltd.

8.  *Aviary.* A large wire mesh cage with covered nesting area, to be supplied and stocked with budgies and canaries, by Hoyle Pet Stores Ltd. This activity is unaffected by the erection of the ticket office.

9.  *Pony rides.* A small cart to be purchased to take children for rides around the farm site.

10. *Disabled ramps.* Ramps to allow wheelchair access to all buildings. This must be finished before the ticket office is in place, because of delivery of concrete.

11. *Picnic barn.* The existing open-sided hay barn is to be filled with picnic tables and benches. Purchased from and delivered by Northgate Garden Centre. These items can be delivered at any time after the yard is finished.

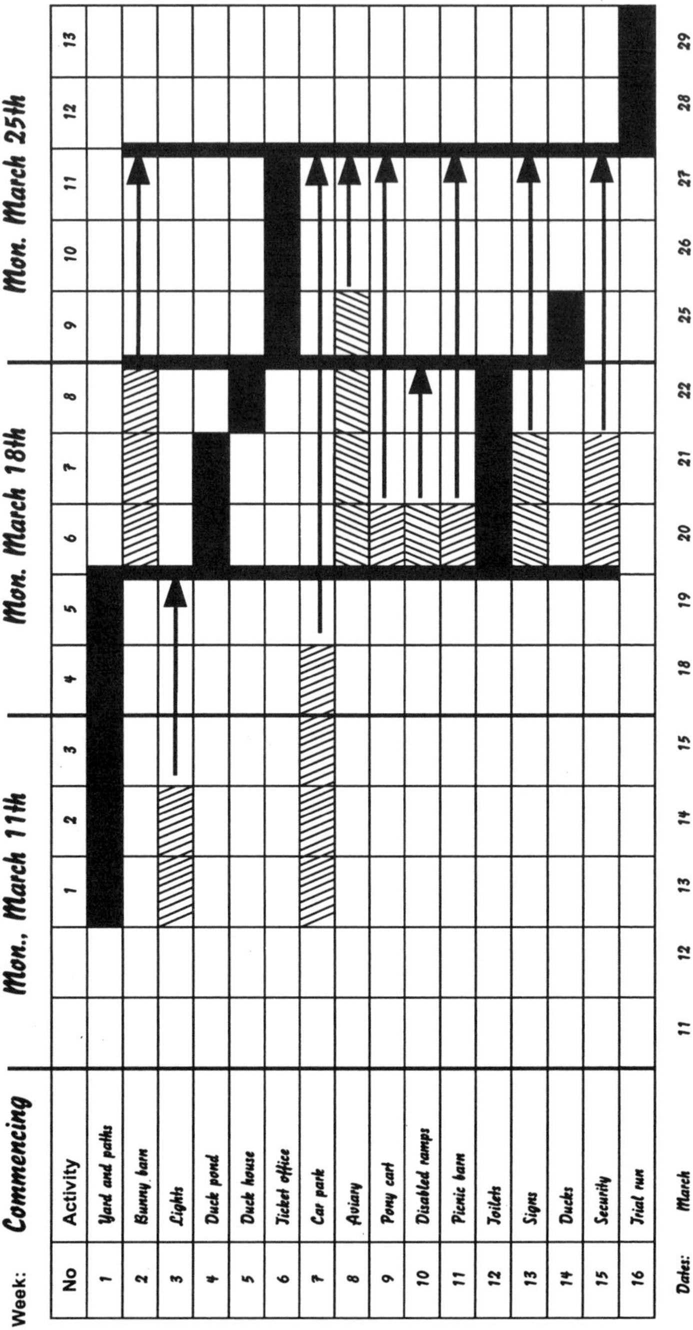


Fig. 32. The Gantt chart for the children's farm.

12. *Toilets.* Temporary toilets will be used during the first twelve months. A unit on a trailer will be hired from Portaflush Cabins. The trailer must arrive before the ticket office is put in place. In addition to bringing in the trailer, the unit must be wired up for electricity and plumbed into the water supply and drains.

13. *Signs.* Signs include a notice at the entrance, direction signs within the farm, and a layout plan on a large board in the yard.

14. *Ducks.* A dozen white Aylesbury ducks will be purchased from the Hoyle livestock market. The market only operates on a Monday. This activity has to be shown as critical on the Gantt chart because it must happen on the Monday.

15. *Security.* Installation of CCTV by the Spyder Eye Security Company.

16. *Trial run.* One day taking staff around the site and explaining duties. Another day when friends and family have a free day out to give staff experience of their duties.

The critical path divides into two parallel paths on day 6. One route is along the pond and duck house activities. The other route is the toilets activity. These must be completed before the ticket office is erected.

### Logging progress

To keep a check on the progress of the project, Bruce uses a progress log. Progress logs are useful for all projects. In this example, the progress log has reached day 8 of the project (22 March). This is illustrated in Figure 33.

Progress log key points are as follows:

• The earliest start and earliest finish dates are the same as those in the CPA network activity boxes and on the Gantt chart – translated into calendar dates.

• Calendar dates are more useful when it comes to logging actual progress.

| No. | Activity | Earliest Start | Earliest Fin. | Actual Start | Actual Fin. | Comments |
|-----|----------|:-----:|:-----:|:-----:|:-----:|----------|
| 1 | Yard and paths | 13/3 | 19/3 | 13/3 | 19/3 | On time |
| 2 | Bunny barn | 20/3 | 22/3 | 20/3 | 22/3 | On time |
| 3 | Lights | 13/3 | 14/3 | 14/3 | 18/3 | Non-critical |
| 4 | Duck pond | 20/3 | 21/3 | 20/3 | 21/3 | On time |
| 5 | Duck house | 22/3 | 22/3 | 22/3 | 22/3 | On time |
| 6 | Ticket office | 25/3 | 27/3 | | | |
| 7 | Car park | 13/3 | 18/3 | 15/3 | | Non-critical |
| 8 | Aviary | 20/3 | 25/3 | | | Start 24/3 |
| 9 | Pony cart | 20/3 | 20/3 | | | Non-critical |
| 10 | Disabled ramps | 20/3 | 20/3 | 20/3 | 20/3 | |
| 11 | Picnic barn | 20/3 | 20/3 | 22/3 | 22/3 | Non-critical |
| 12 | Toilets | 20/3 | 22/3 | 21/3 | | Delivered |
| 13 | Signs | 20/3 | 21/3 | | | Non-critical |
| 14 | Ducks | 25/3 | 25/3 | | | Monday only |
| 15 | Security | 20/3 | 21/3 | 22/3 | | Non-critical |
| 16 | Trial run | 28/3 | 29/3 | | | Critical |

Fig. 33. The children's farm project progress log.

## Dealing with difficulties
The case study project has gone to plan, up to day 5. But at this point Bruce identifies some problems.

*Activities 2 and 8 – bunny barn and aviary*
Hoyle Pet Stores has insufficient staff to work on these two activities simultaneously. Hoyle Pet Stores agrees to start the aviary on Saturday 24th. This extra day allows the activity to be completed by the 27th.

*Activity 12 – the toilets*
A one-day strike occurs at Portaflush Cabins on Wednesday 20th, the day the toilets were due to be delivered. They are delivered the following day. This looks like a significant problem, because the activity is on the critical path.

However, once the toilets have been delivered, the ticket office can be installed. The remaining two days of activity 12 are the electrical and plumbing work. So this one day's delay has not been a problem in practice.

## Opening the farm
There are no other problems with the case study project. The trial run takes place on 28 and 29 March. Woods Children's Farm opens for business on Saturday 30 March.

## MANAGING CHANGE

Taking action to get a project back on track usually involves making changes. In the children's farm case study, the changes made during the project were relatively minor. In larger, more complex projects, changes may be significant enough to require authority before they can be made.

The steps of the change process are illustrated in Figure 34.

## Evaluating change
At the heart of the change process is the evaluation of the proposed change to the project. The evaluation will:

- act as a self-check for the Project Manager, to ensure he or she has considered all the implications of the proposed change.

- provide the necessary information to the person or group of people who will grant authority for the change.

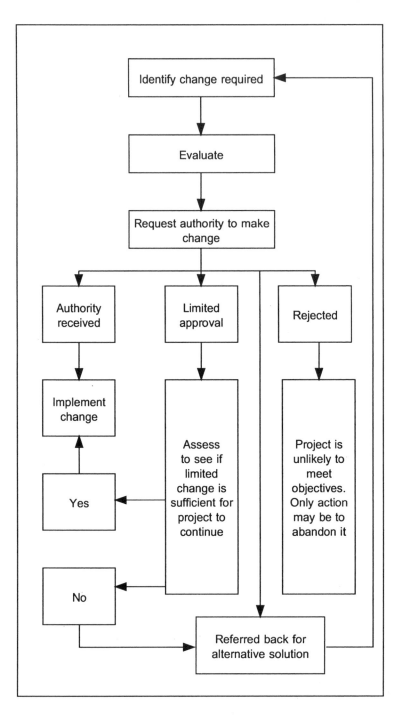

Fig. 34. The project change process.

100

*Evaluation questions*
The following questions are suggested as a method of evaluating the proposed change:

1.  Is the change actually possible to make?
2.  How will the change affect progress?
3.  How much will the change cost?
4.  Who will pay for the change?
5.  Will any scrap material result from the change?
6.  Will the changes have to be backdated?
7.  Will there be any reduction in the quality of the outcome of the project?
8.  What paperwork and plans will have to be amended?
9.  Are there any safety implications that would result from making the change?

## Documenting the change policy

For companies who undertake a lot of project work, the company project change policy should be documented. This is necessary to clarify:

• What are the cost limits that require authority?

• Who is able to authorise changes?

• What happens to the project if changes are rejected?

• Is the planning of a new project to replace the existing project allowed, when change is not possible, or rejected?

## Controlling the paperwork

Implementing a change to bring a project back on track is likely to mean an update to one or all of the following documents:

• CPA network diagram
• Gantt chart
• cost estimate.

To ensure the right people are holding the correct paperwork, a document control process should be used. There are three essential features of a document control process:

1.  *An issue status* – on the project document.

This consists of the issue number and the date of issue of the document.
Example: Issue 1. 17 Nov. 199X.

2.  *A distribution list* – which details who holds the document, and its issue status. A suitable style for a distribution list is illustrated in Figure 35.

3.  *Confirmation of receipt* – arranged by a suitable method, for example:

    – delivery by hand
    – use e-mail
    – ask recipient to telephone or fax on receipt of the document.

The dates of receipt are marked on the distribution list, as in the example illustrated in Figure 35.

---

**Project title:**     Garden Centre          No: JD/CK/203/9X

**Project manager:**    Clark Kelly

**Distribution list for:** Gantt chart

|  | Issue 1<br>17 Nov 9X | Issue 2<br>14 Jan 9X | Issue 3 |
|---|---|---|---|
| Keith Robins | 18/11 | 14/1 | |
| Ken Marley | 19/11 | 16/1 | |
| Vikki Parker | 18/11 | 14/1 | |
| Michael Curtis | 20/11 | 15/1 | |
| Rebecca Morgan | 21/11 | 15/1 | |
| Susan Birch | 18/11 | 14/1 | |

Fig. 35. A distribution list for controlling project documents.

## SUMMARY OF KEY POINTS

### Keeping the project under control
1. Monitor by measuring progress.
2. Control by taking action.

### Measuring progress
1. A progress reporting process must be in place as soon as the work starts.
2. Information can be gathered by regular reports.
3. Project Manager should view progress by visiting site where work is being done.
4. A progress log can be used to track progress.
5. Project Manager should specify reporting method.
6. An overall project report may be required based on collated information.

### Taking action
1. The Project Manager decides on whether to take action – not individual team members.
2. Action involving change may require authority.
3. Project documents may have to be updated when action is taken.

### Managing change
1. Company project change policy should be documented.
2. The proposed change should be evaluated before requesting authority to implement change.
3. Project documents must be properly controlled – with an issue status and distribution list.

## CASE STUDIES

### Albert's eyes are closed when his dream fails
Albert, a 50-year-old supervisor at a car assembly plant, takes early retirement. The redundancy package is generous. In addition to the lump sum and pension, there is an offer of free training to help people find new jobs. Albert chooses a Project Management course.

Albert then buys a large run-down house in a coastal resort seventy miles away. Using his recently acquired Project Management skills, he intends to convert the house into a holiday hotel. When he plans the project, the finish date is in good time for the start of the summer holiday season.

Albert has all the necessary skills to be a Project Manager, except that he is too trusting of the building company doing the work. Albert believes the weekly progress reports he receives over the phone. And he does not appreciate the need to go and see what's going on for himself.

The work gets well behind schedule, and Albert only finds out when the hotel should be ready to open. It is now too close to the holiday season to take the necessary action to put things right. Albert is forced to sell the half-finished hotel, to pay off the large bank loan he took out to finance the project.

## Limited approval, but objectives are still achieved

Hoyle Technology College is installing a new computer system in its library. This will be used to manage book loans and to provide students with reference information.

Barbara, one of the college lecturers, is managing the project, with all the work subcontracted to an experienced computer supplier – Jess Micro Systems.

Barbara monitors the work by daily visits to the team of engineers. She is not content with just talking to the supervisor. She gets a clearer picture of what's going on from the men actually doing the work.

Halfway through the work, a practical difficulty arises. There is insufficient room in the cable ducts, from the library to the mainframe computer, at the other end of the building.

Another route is found for the cables: up the service risers, then through the roof space. This means additional expenditure for the longer cables. Also there are safety implications for the engineers working in the loft without a proper floor.

The college manager gives limited approval. As many cables as possible are to be run through the ducts, with only those that can't be fitted in to be routed through the roof space. Jess Micro Systems are also asked to provide crawling boards, to ensure the safety of their workforce while working in the loft.

Barbara implements this action, and the new computer system is up and running on time.

## Tracking the delegates with frequent phone calls

The management of the Midvale Building Society decides it would be a good idea to hold a series of one-day team-building events for all their employees. The Midvale has recently taken over the

Perrydown Society, and the integration of staff has been noticeably poor.

The team-building event is organised using Project Management. A large number of identical events will be run in various parts of the country spread over several days. This means that Society counters will not be depleted of too many staff.

Planning has to be meticulous, to ensure everyone gets to the right event, and that each event runs to time. Phone calls to the venues allow the project team to check everything required for the event is to hand the day before. In addition, the project team receives faxes of the names of the people who have arrived for the event, for cross-checking against the invitation lists.

There are places reserved on mop-up events, for those who have missed their booking because of sickness or other reasons. At the close of the project, all employees have attended an event.

A month after the finish of the project, a survey by questionnaire is undertaken. The results indicate that the improvement in team working has exceeded the project objective.

## DISCUSSION POINTS

1.  Look at the flowchart for the change process, illustrated in Figure 34. Verify that this process can be placed inside the action box of the monitor and control process, illustrated in Figure 28.

2.  Activity 12, in the children's farm case study, was to deliver and install the toilets. Separating the delivery from the installation solved the problem over the one-day delay. Would the Gantt chart have been very different if two separate activities had been planned?

3.  A project team is to meet monthly. On the agenda there is an item for *Review of Progress*. Why is it better for the members to send in progress reports in advance, rather than to wait for individuals to report verbally at the meeting?

# 6
# Employing a Computer

## ASSISTING THE PROJECT MANAGER

There are several personal computer (PC) software packages available to assist the Project Manager.

### Clarifying what software can do

Before we look at how to use Project Manager software, here are some important points:

- The software is only a tool – it can't replace the Project Manager.

- It is not the software that creates the project plans, it is the Project Manager.

- The software needs accurate information to be effective.

- The Project Manager needs to understand basic Project Management techniques in order to use the software effectively.

### Considering the need for software

For simple projects, like the case studies for the office move and children's farm, traditional pen and paper methods are cost effective and efficient.

Software packages become viable when managing:

- *More than 20 projects per year.* The cost of buying the software spread over 20 projects will not be significant compared with all the other planning costs. If your company has a licence to operate the software throughout its organisation, 20 projects per year applies to the total for all users.

- *Projects with 20 or more activities.* When projects have 20 or more activities, Gantt charts become difficult to manage using traditional techniques. The situation is made more complicated if changes to plans are made. Software can cope with both of these issues very effectively.

## Adding up the advantages

The advantages gained when using software in Project Management are as follows:

1. *Flexibility.* Changes to project plans can be made instantly.

2. *Information.* Software can rapidly produce up-to-date printed reports, charts, lists, *etc.* The information can also be edited to be specific to a person or a department.

3. *Templating.* Refer back to the security company case study at the end of Chapter 3. They used a checklist to assist the planning process, because a lot of the activities were common across different projects. Some software packages have the facility to hold **templates** covering the common activities. The appropriate templates can then be called up and re-used, which saves repeating work already done on previous projects.

4. *Linking.* It is possible to link PCs by a network to provide an integrated Project Management system for your company. This means all the company projects can be scheduled together and make the best use of resources.

## Going for software

If you are intending to use Project Management software, you will need:

1. *A personal computer (PC).*

2. *A decent printer.* Project Management will always depend on printed information being available where the work is being done.

3. *Suitable accommodation.* Because paper is still involved, room will be required to lay plans out on a desk or table.

In addition to the above, the following additional item may be required:

4. *Large sheet plotter.* If you use an A4 printer for large projects you will have to stick a number of separate sheets together to see the whole plan. A large sheet plotter will print the plan on a single piece of paper.

## USING PROJECT MANAGEMENT SOFTWARE

To demonstrate how Project Management software is used, a simple case study has been chosen, with thirteen activities.

### Restoring the pottery

Hoyle Bank Pottery operated until the 1930s, specialising in large decorative terracotta garden pots and containers. A local business-man has decided to open a modern pottery, under the Hoyle Bank name, and to work to the original patterns and designs.

The new pottery will be located ten miles from the original site, in a refurbished warehouse next to Hadlow railway station. The clay will be bought in from a specialist supplier, rather than using the traditional local clay.

### Sorting out the dependencies

Project Management software is only as good as the information that is fed into it. It will not be able to sort out for itself that the old warehouse building needs a new roof, before the floor can be skimmed with concrete to make it level.

The Project Manager must specify the dependencies, if the Gantt chart is to be a realistic and practical plan.

Refer to the project planning process, illustrated in Figure 27. The software takes over in the right-hand vertical line of boxes – from: 'Construct CPA network' down to and including 'Adjust CPA network'. However, it is still under the control of the Project Manager.

### Planning with software

The Gantt chart for the pottery case study, using a typical software package, is illustrated in Figure 36.

To produce this Gantt chart, information was input to the PC as follows:

1.   Activities listed with their durations.

2.   Activities linked according to dependencies.

The Gantt chart appears as the information is input. This means the CPA network is effectively bypassed. However, it is possible to ask the PC for a network diagram to be printed, after the Gantt chart has been constructed.

## Displaying the information

There will be a number of different display options for the Gantt chart. In the Gantt chart illustrated in Figure 36, the start and finish dates for each activity are at the ends of the bars. However, this is just one option and the dates don't have to be displayed in this form.

The Gantt chart on the PC screen will be displayed in different colours; for example, blue for non-critical paths, red for critical paths. If you have a black and white printer, you should be able to change the colours and shading of the bars to allow the critical path to stand out.

## Summarising activities

With most software packages, you will be able to group activities under common headings. For example, in the case study, *Roof*, *Windows* and *Internal walls* could be summarised as a single *Building work* activity.

This is the same as stepping back up the work breakdown structure to the previous higher level. It is a useful feature for large projects. Senior managers will only want to see a summarised version of the project activities on a single sheet of A4 paper, not a huge sheet of hundreds of activities.

## Plotting progress

In the Gantt chart illustrated in Figure 36, the dark bars along the centres of activities 1, 2 and 3 show the progress. Activities 1 and 2 are completed. Activity 3 is 50 per cent complete.

The *Roof* activity is on the critical path. The critical path is indicated by darker bars, but the software has made the dark *Roof* activity bar lighter, to show up the progress bar.

This would not have been a problem with a colour printer. When you look at the software on offer you should try to find as much out about it as possible before buying it. Small points like this may cause you difficulties when you actually come to use it.

## Tracking resources

One of the other useful features that is likely to be included with the software is a method of recording and plotting the progress of costs and resources for each of the activities.

## Making changes

Changes to the Gantt chart can be made instantly; for example, adding an extra day to the duration of an activity. Remember,

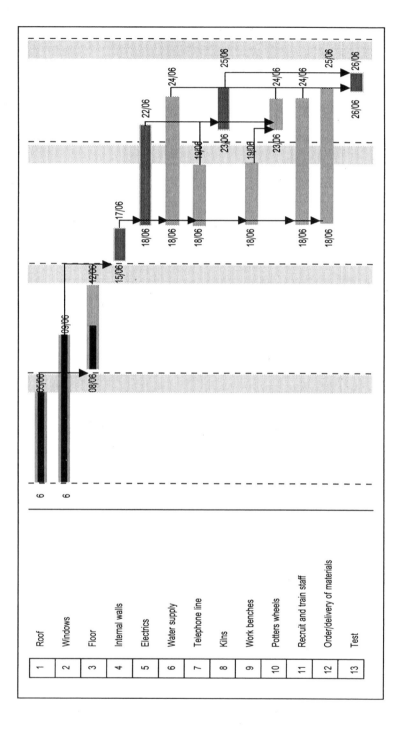

Fig. 36. Gantt chart using typical Project Manager software.

however, to print a copy of the original before making the changes, if you require it for reference purposes. It will be lost as soon as the new information is input.

## TRAINING YOURSELF TO USE SOFTWARE

Most software will come with a **tutor** as part of the package. With some software you can bring up an **information card** on the screen alongside your plans, to help guide you through the correct steps.

### Getting to know your software
Here is a suggested list of key steps to help you to get to know how to use your Project Management software.

1. Use a case study or a real situation with less than twenty activities.

2. Draw the work breakdown structure on paper.

3. Allocate durations.

4. Sort out dependencies.

5. Draw out a CPA network.

6. Draw a Gantt chart. (You may be able to miss out step 5 if you have had a lot of experience with drawing Gantts.)

7. Use the information from steps 2, 3 and 4 as the input to the Project Management software.

8. Produce the software version of the Gantt chart.

9. Compare results of 6 and 8. You should have the same information about the project displayed in chart form.

## CHOOSING YOUR SOFTWARE

There are more than a dozen Project Management software packages available for you to use on your PC. However, your company may already have Project Management software. It may also have a licence which allows employees in the company to copy the package from one PC to another. In these situations you should obtain a copy of the company's preferred software.

However, if you're starting from scratch, there are a number of points to consider when choosing software for yourself.

## Trying out some software

If possible, you should have a play with the Project Management software on a PC belonging to a friend or colleague. Try it with one of the case studies from this book; for example, the exhibition in Chapter 4, or the children's farm in Chapter 5.

*Note*: Upgrades to software are made available from time to time, so make sure you check which **version** it is you're using. It might be different from the software with the same name, currently on the shelves at computer stores.

## Looking at the reports

The most costly stage in a project is when the work is being done – the produce stage. So it is important that the plans and reports produced by the software are the most suitable for the people who are doing the work.

Study examples of the plans and reports on offer from a number of different software packages, to see which meet your requirements.

Other considerations should be:

- What reports would senior mangers find the most informative?

- How does progress reporting work?

## Training the user

A **tutor** or **self-teach package** that comes with the software must be easy to follow. For more complex Project Management software, formal training run by the software supplier may be necessary. You will need to find out if the training is included in the purchase price, or if it is an additional cost.

## Supporting the users

You should find out about the guarantee that comes with the software, and about maintenance beyond the guarantee period.

Also verify if there is technical back-up available, such as a help desk number to ring if you're having problems getting the software to work properly.

## Making sense of error messages

If you're looking at software that generates error messages, check that they are easy to understand. If they don't seem to make sense, then you're likely to get into a muddle if you make a mistake while using the software.

## Templating projects

If **templating** is a feature that is useful to your type of project work, you will need to buy software that has this facility.

## Working with a network

If you're intending to have an integrated Project Management system with linked PCs, then ensure that the software on offer has this capability.

## Shopping for Project Management software

Project Management software needs to be chosen carefully. The following points should be noted:

- Price is *not* a good indication of performance.

- Information in adverts should *not* be taken too seriously.

- Good reviews in computer journals are *not* a reliable guide to how the software will perform in the hands of an experienced Project Manager.

- Packages described as 'powerful' may work well with small projects, but perform badly with large projects.

- Buying software that does not meet expectations can be an expensive mistake, both in the purchase price and in the time wasted trying to use it.

## SHOPPING CHECKLIST

Here is a checklist to use as a guide when buying Project Management software.

1.  Ask what your friends and colleagues use.

2.  Buy a computer magazine that contains plenty of adverts for PCs and software outlets.

3.  Call in to the software outlets, or telephone them if they are just mail order.

4.  From as many software outlets as possible, obtain the following:

    – what their best selling Project Management software package is

    – what they think would best suit your needs
    – the names and addresses of the software suppliers
    – a catalogue and price list.

5.  Make a judgement as to what you think the most suitable
    package might be for your situation, taking into account the
    price and all the other information gathered so far.

6.  Contact the software supplier, and ask for details about the
    software you are thinking of buying. Ask about:

    – the performance of the chosen software in relation to your
      type of project work
    – the range and style of reports
    – the need for a colour printer
    – training requirements for the user
    – the guarantee and technical support
    – error messages
    – templating
    – suitability for networking.

7.  If you are not satisfied by the answers given by the supplier,
    then go back to step 5.

8.  Go round the loop as many times as required, until you're
    confident that you've made the right choice.

*Note*
You should still ask about templating and networking, even if these
are facilities you don't require. You could end up paying for them as
part of the package, even if you don't need them.

## CASE STUDIES

### Bringing the town back to life
Ness Park is an historic market town which has been in decline for a
number of years. The local people don't bother to use the shops,
they prefer to go to the out-of-town supermarket.

With the reopening of the Hadlow Branch Line Railway, the
council is sure that Ness Park can be brought back to life.

Market Square is surrounded by historic buildings. These are to
be restored and the empty shops let for cafés, a tourist information
office, souvenir shops and other attractions.

The local development corporation draws up a programme of

projects for the restoration of the individual buildings. They use a software package which allows the projects to be linked as an integrated Project Management system. A template is used which includes all the basic building work common to each of the projects.

Weekly summary plans are printed, indicating the progress of the work. These are displayed for the general public, on the notice-board outside the market hall.

Work is completed on time, and Ness Park is soon attracting a large number of tourists. The local people now feel proud of their town, and they begin to use the market and other shops again.

### Software rescues museum plans from dry rot

The Hadlow Branch Line Railway has been offered an extensive collection of pre-war 0-gauge model railway engines, rolling stock, track and buildings. There is just one condition. The collection must be put on display for visitors to enjoy.

The director of the railway, David Mitchell-Jones, thinks the solution is to acquire the signal box that has been planned for some time. They would then use this as a model railway museum.

Laura is asked to be the Project Manager. She suggests it is about time the company invested in a Project Management software package, as projects have become a regular feature of life at the railway. Laura buys a software package she has already used. She has been on a Project Management course as part of her full-time job with the district council.

As the project gets underway, there is an unexpected problem. The signal box earmarked for recovery and transport to the site is found to have dry rot and it can't be moved. To get round this problem, the project team decide to have a replica signal box built on site.

With the flexibility of the Project Manager software, the plans are quickly revised, and the project recovers from this set-back. The museum opens on time and it proves to be a very popular attraction for visitors.

### Software is on the menu at Phil's café

Philip, a software engineer who has recently been made redundant, is to open a café in one of the refurbished buildings in Ness Park Market Square. This will be an Internet Café, with PCs provided for customers who want to drop in for a coffee and to spend time surfing the Internet. It will also act as an advice centre for users of PCs.

Phil shops around for a Project Management software package to suit his café project. He takes his time over the choice of software. He contacts several suppliers, and asks them to send technical descriptions of their packages. He also visits Laura, who often acts as Project Manager for the Hadlow Branch Line Railway. They have recently purchased some software, and Phil wants to see how this performs.

With all the available information, Phil is able to make a sensible choice. He then plans his café on paper using traditional Project Management techniques, before he tries out the software. This approach ensures his understands the basics, and he also has something to compare the performance of the software against.

After the café is opened, Phil keeps all the project paperwork plus the files on his PC. This proves very useful as demonstration material when customers come in for advice about Project Management using software packages.

## DISCUSSION POINTS

1.  What sort of companies or projects might benefit from having the template facility as part of their Project Management software?

2.  How can the wrong choice of Project Management software cause serious difficulties for a company or project?

3.  Imagine you're in charge of planning a large country fair each year. What advantages would there be in using a Project Management software package?

# 7
# Finishing Off the Work

## CLOSING THE PROJECT

When the work has been completed, the project moves from the produce stage to the close stage. Refer back to the illustration in Figure 3 for a reminder of the project life cycle.

### Limiting expenditure

During the produce stage, charges for the work will have been submitted. Sending in timesheets is a typical method. The cost of the work will have been allocated to the project number, or to the individual project activity codes.

Projects are formally closed to ensure no further expenditure is booked against them. When the workforce moves on to a new project, charges need to be allocated to the new activities.

### Reaching the end

The project is closed when it reaches the end point. This is when **the project output matches the project deliverables**.

The project deliverables are:

- specified in the client requirements
- what should be *seen* when all the work has been done
- separate and different from the objectives.

Look back at the client requirements for the railway extension case study, illustrated in Figure 7. One of the key deliverables was a half-hourly train service. This, and all the other case study deliverables, fits the key points listed above.

### Reporting closure

The Project Manager formally closes the project by issuing a closure report. The suggested  contents of a closure report are as follows:

1.  *Project title.*

2.  *Project number.*

3.  *Project Manager.*

4.  *Client.*

5.  *Closure date.*

6.  *Reason for closure.* This usually means that the deliverables listed in the client requirements have all been met.

7.  *Special instructions.* For example, the procedures that will take over after the closure.

8.  *Authority to close.* Client's signature and date.

9.  *Distribution.* All the people and departments who need to know the project has closed.

## LEARNING FOR THE FUTURE

All projects have **objectives** which are:

* the expected benefits to be gained as a result of undertaking the project
* the reason why the project is to be undertaken
* separate and different from the deliverables.

Look back at the client requirements for the railway extension case study, illustrated in Figure 7. All the objectives fit the key points listed above; for example, making the railway profitable.

After a project has finished, we need to check that the objectives have been met.

### Undertaking a review

To check that project objectives have been met, a project review is undertaken. However, the project review does more than just verify that the promised benefits have been gained. It also examines how well the project was run, so that the management of future projects can be improved.

The suggested contents of a project review are as follows:

1.  *Project title.*

2.  *Project number*.

3.  *Project Manager*

4.  *Client*.

5.  *Closure date*.

6.  *Review date*.

7.  *Achievements*. The benefits gained compared to the project objectives.

8.  *Financial performance*. Cost of project compared to estimated cost.

9.  *Change requests*. Details of any changes submitted for authority, to bring the project back on track.

10. *Organisation*. How well did the team work together? How effective was the monitoring of progress? Suggestions for similar future projects.

11. *Methods*. Were the planning methods suitable? Would there be advantages doing it differently next time?

12. *Distribution*. Typically the project team, senior managers and people who have benefited from the project.

### Combining closure and review

The first five headings of the closure report and the project review are identical. For some projects it will be possible to combine the two into a single project closure and review report.

For most projects, however, the review must happen some time after the project is closed. Look back at the example of the customer service centre project, illustrated in Figure 1. The deliverables are the items listed in the *end* box of the flowchart, but the benefits are to be measured by monitoring the centre performance, for one month after the opening date. This means that the review can't take place sooner than one month after the closure report.

### RECORDING THE RESULTS

Let's use a case study to see how project closure and review works in practice.

**Recruiting lots of people**

Addmore Personal Insurance have opened a new national Call Centre. This Centre has taken over all the sales work from the local offices.

Teams of advisers telephone potential customers. They are told about the range and benefits of the various insurance services, with a view to signing customers up to one of the schemes on offer.

The case study project is *The Recruitment and Training of the Call Centre Staff*. Details of the project are as follows:

*Client*
The Centre Director, Bradley Hirst, an experienced Call Centre Manager, brought over from the USA.

*Project Manager*
Julia Forsyth, the Centre's personnel manager.

*Deliverables*
Specified in the client requirements as follows:

- Opening date – 1 September.

- 20 team managers.

- 15 advisers per team.

- Managers trained to standard skills list:
  - system operation
  - call monitoring techniques
  - staff personal development
  - managing people
  - health and safety.

- Advisers trained to standard skills list:
  - system operation
  - sales techniques
  - range of products and services
  - customer care skills.

*Objectives*
Specified in the client requirements as follows:

- Calling rate and sales conversion rate at the end of month one to be 12 calls/hour and 7 per cent. (Conversion rate is the percentage of the people contacted who agree to sign up to a scheme.)

- All advisers to have had four of their calls monitored by their manager by 30 September.

- Information from call monitoring to have been fed into personal development plans for each adviser and personal targets set, by 30 September.

## Opening the Call Centre
The Call Centre will open for business, with all the trained staff and managers in position, on 1 September. This means *The Recruitment and Training Project* can be formally closed on 31 August. The case study closure report is illustrated in Figure 37.

## Learning from the recruitment project
The project objectives are very clear about what the fully trained Call Centre staff are expected to achieve. Targets have been set for the performance of the Centre at the end of month one. So the best time to undertake the project review is 1 October, when the Project Manager can look back at the achievements of the first month of operation.

Although it is unlikely the company will run another recruitment project of this type, there will still be a lot of valuable learning points for other projects. So how well the project was run will also be an important part of the review.

The project review for the case study is illustrated in Figure 38.

## Reviewing with the team
The project review should involve the members of the project team. The best approach is to have an additional project team meeting, just to cover the project review.

## FILING PROJECT PAPERWORK

After the project has been formally closed, and the project review completed, all the paperwork should be kept in the project file. The suggested contents list for project files is illustrated in Figure 10.

## Building up a library
A central library holding the files of completed projects allows people access to information that can be useful for other projects.

# ADDMORE PERSONAL INSURANCE
## PROJECT CLOSURE REPORT

**Project**: Call Centre Staff Recruitment and Training

**No**: API 3/2      Project manager: Julia Forsyth

**Client**: Bradley Hirst – Centre Director

**Project closure date**: 31 August 199X

**Reason for closure**:

The following items are in place –

  Ready for business on 1 September, at 0900 hrs

  20 team managers

  20 teams of 15 advisers

  Managers trained to standard skills list

  Advisers trained to standard skills list

**Special instructions**:

Team will operate to Call Centre Procedures –

  API 10 *Team Manager's Guide and Responsibilities*

  API 11 *Advisers Guide and Responsibilities*

These instructions include Call Monitoring and Personal Development.

**Authority to close the project**

This project is formally closed. No further expenditure may be booked against it.

**Signed**: *Bradley Hirst*      *31/8/9X*

**Distribution**:

  Project File        (original copy)

  Bradley Hirst       Centre Director

  Stephen Quinn       Training Manager

  Paul Carter         Centre Resource Manager

Fig. 37. A project closure report.

Features of the library should be:

- an indexing system that allows files to be located from their title and/or project number

- one person have the responsibility for running the library, to ensure it is always up to date and tidy

- a loans procedure so that people can sign for and borrow files

- a retention policy, so that files which are no longer relevant can be weeded out (typically two years retention)

- an archiving process for information that must be held longer for legal or other reasons; for example, electronic storage or the company main archive.

### Disposing of surplus paperwork

During the project, people on the distribution lists will have gathered a considerable amount of paperwork. With a copy of the project file in the library, there is no need for anyone to hold on to the paperwork of completed projects, so they should be encouraged to dispose of surplus paperwork, and to use the library for future referencing.

### SUMMARY OF KEY POINTS

### When the project is closed
1. Project will have achieved the deliverables.
2. A closure report is issued, authorised by the client.
3. No further expenditure can be booked to that project.

### The project review
1. Details of the review are recorded in a project review report.
2. The purpose of the review is to check that the objectives have been achieved.
3. It also covers other items:
   - financial performance
   - number of changes
   - how well the project was organised
   - the methods used.
4. The review usually involves the project team.

# ADDMORE PERSONAL INSURANCE
# PROJECT REVIEW REPORT

**Project**: Call Centre Staff Recruitment and Training
**No**: API 3/2     **Project Manager**: Julia Forsyth
**Client**: Bradley Hirst – Centre Director
**Project closure date**: 31 August 199X
**Project review date**: 1 October 199X
**Achievements**:

|  | Calls/hour | Conversion rate |
|---|---|---|
| Target | 12.0 | 7.0% |
| Actual | 12.4 | 6.8% |

Refresher training has been arranged for the advisers. This will emphasise the need to spend more time on each call and improve selling techniques.

*Call monitoring*
98% completed. Shortfall due to sick leave.

*Personal development*
Personal targets set for 80% of advisers. Managers have been advised that 100% must be achieved by the end of next month.

**Financial performance**:
Project underspent by 5% against original feasibility estimate, due to lower than expected advertising costs.

**Change requests**:
No requests for authority to make changes to the project were submitted.
**Organisation**:
The project team worked well together. There does not appear to be the need to have a permanent Project Manager post at the Centre.
**Methods**:
Manually planned with pen and paper. Suggest Centre should invest in a Project Management software package for future projects.
**Project Manager's authorisation**

*Julia Forsyth* . . . . . . . . . . . *1/10/9X* . .

**Distribution**:
Copies of this review to:
Project file (original copy)
Project team members
Call Centre Director
Call Centre Team Managers

Fig. 38. A project review report.

**Retention of records**
1. Retain the files of closed projects in a central library.
2. Encourage people to dispose of surplus paperwork.

## CASE STUDIES

### Time wasting muddle could have been avoided
The Hadlow Branch Line Railway has proved to be very profitable, since it was extended through to Ness Park.

To make the management of the large number of volunteer workers more efficient, it was decided to open a new office. There would be a manager and a secretary to run this side of the business. They would be located on the first floor of the heritage centre, next door to the director's office.

The creation of the new office, and the recruitment of the manager and secretary, was run as a project.

Some time after the office was opened, the company accountant noticed that the charges for painting and decorating the office were unusually high. But there was a simple explanation.

Following on from the office job, the contractors were employed to paint the whole of the hostel area. The contractor was not concerned about where his money came from, and he continued to charge the company against the office project.

This charging muddle took the accountant some time to sort out. There would not have been a problem if the office project had been formally closed, to prevent any further expenditure being booked against it.

### John educates himself in Project Management
John has resigned from his job at a large London book publisher, to work for himself. He starts by buying an existing small publishing company, Bedside Education, which specialises in Education and the Arts.

John uses Project Management to organise the takeover. On completion, he writes a brief closure report. This verifies that the deliverables have been met; for example, change of address on the stationery, and all authors contacted.

Six months after the project ends, John undertakes a project review. This confirms that the expected financial benefits have been achieved. John is also planning to buy another publisher, so the information in the project file will help to further improve the process for the next takeover.

## Ken's trip to the past helps with his plans

*The Lost Planet* Appreciation Society has experienced a revival in interest, due to the original series being repeated on Cable TV.

The Society decides to organise a conference in London for its world-wide fans. This will consist of displays of the props used in the filming, talks by the writers and stars, and sales of clothing and souvenirs.

Ken, the Appreciation Society Chairman, has only had this job for twelve months, but he knows there was a similar conference runs five years ago in Manchester.

Ken finds the project file for the Manchester conference in the Society's archives. The objectives and deliverables for the previous conference are almost identical to those for the London conference. The project review is also very helpful, because it highlights all the mistakes made during the first project.

Using the information in the project file as a guide, Ken is able to plan and run a highly successful London conference.

### CHECKLIST

- At the client requirements stage, at the start of a project, setting realistic *objectives* and *deliverables*, ensures the project closure and review are straightforward and meaningful.

- The *time*, *cost* and *quality* relationship, illustrated in Figure 2, is a helpful but an inaccurate representation of project objectives. Finishing the project on *time*, and within *cost* estimates, are to do with the project itself. But *quality* is related to the benefits the project will deliver to the client.

- Without an effective filing system, and a retention policy, companies holding a large number of project files, will find it difficult to make use of the experience gained from previous projects.

# Glossary

**Activity**. Also known as a work package. A self-contained parcel of work, attributable to one person, a team of people, or a subcontractor.

**Activity list**. A list of project activities. All the work that must be done to complete the project. The final set of boxes in a work breakdown structure.

**Arrow diagram**. A method of scheduling project work, similar to CPA network analysis. (Not described in this book.)

**Business case**. A formal submission, from the Project Manager to the client, requesting authority for the project expenditure.

**Client**. The person the project is run for. The person who sets the project objectives.

**Closure report**. A document authorised by the client, to formally close the project, when it reaches the end point. This prevents any further expenditure being booked against the project.

**Critical path**. Activities lying on the critical path, in a CPA network, must start and finish on time, if the project is to remain on schedule.

**Critical Path Analysis (CPA)**. Scheduling the activities in a network diagram, to ascertain their start and finish dates.

**Deliverables**. The measurable output of a project. Specified as part of the client's requirements.

**Dependency table**. The activity list, plus information showing the activities which must be completed, before subsequent activities can start.

**Document control**. A method of ensuring that the people involved in a project have the correct issues of paperwork.

**Gantt chart**. A bar chart which illustrates activity start and finish dates, dependencies, critical path and total floats.

**Network diagram**. Activities are depicted as boxes, with links between them, to indicate the order in which activities must be done.

**Objectives**. The benefits that will result from undertaking the project. The reason why the project is being done. Specified as part of the client's requirements.

**PERT**. Stands for Programme Evaluation and Review Technique. Similar to CPA network analysis, but not covered in this book. The names PERT and CPA are often interchanged, and you may find PERT used to describe parts of some Project Management software.

**PRINCE**. (Not covered in this book.) Stands for PRojects IN Controlled Environment. A structured Project Management philosophy. Companies have to work to PRINCE when undertaking projects for government departments. There are PRINCE-related software packages available.

**Programme**. A group of related but separate projects, linked together in an overall programme.

**Project life cycle**. From the start point, to the end point, a project goes through four stages: Initiate, Specify, Produce and Close. The Produce stage is when the work is being done and most of the money is being spent.

**Project Management software**. Personal computer software packages are available to assist the Project Manager to plan and run projects. These do not replace the skills of the Project Manager. A good knowledge of Project Management methods is required to get the most out of the software.

**Project Manager**. The person who manages the project and plans most of the detail. Selection of the right kind of person is the key to successful Project Management.

**Project team**. The people who report to the Project Manager, assist with the planning, undertake some of the work, and/or supervise others doing the work.

**Quality**. Together with time and cost, quality completes the overall picture of the project objectives. Quality needs to be thought of as 'meeting customer expectations', rather a gold-plated requirement in all cases.

**Review report**. Produced by the Project Manager after the project has closed, to check that the objectives have been met. Also provides information helpful for the running of future projects.

**Standard activity box**. In CPA networks, all activity boxes have an identical layout, with pigeon holes for time and date information.

**Subcontractors**. People or organisations who are not part of the project team, but who undertake some of the project work. They can be company employees or external to the company.

**Total float**. The amount of time an activity can shift, without it affecting the project.

**Work breakdown structure**. The method of subdividing the project work, by means of a mother and daughter family tree, to produce the activity list.

# Further Reading

*Managing Projects* is intended as a complete guide to Project Management. Practice and involvement with projects are the keys to success, rather than further academic studies. However, the following books are suggested as being helpful in providing a wider view of Project Management, for those who wish to explore the subject further.

*Project Management*, Dennis Lock (Gower, 6th edition, 1996).
*Project Management*, Harvey Maylor (Pitman Publishing, 1996).
*Project Management and Project Network Techniques*, Keith Lockyer and James Gordon (Pitman Publishing, 1996).

# Useful Addresses

Association for Project Management. 85 Oxford Road, High Wycombe, Buckinghamshire HP11 2DX. Tel: (01494) 440090. Publishes *Project* and *International Journal of Project Managers*. Arranges seminars and meetings. There is also a certification procedure for members of the Association, which provides evidence of competence as a Project Manager.

Central Computer & Telecommunications Agency (CCTA), Rosebery Court, St Andrews Business Park, Norwich NR7 0HS. Tel: (01603) 704704. Advice available for Project Management in the public sector.

PRINCE User Group Ltd, Forest House, The Metro Centre, Toutley Road, Wokingham, Berkshire RG41 1QW. Tel: (01189) 795640. for further information about managing projects with PRINCE.

# Index

Activity, 47, 49, 109
Activity list, 47, 49
Archives, 123
Arrow diagram, 64

Ballpark estimate, 25
Bar chart, 78
Business case, 53

Calendar dates, 90, 97
Change process, 93, 99, 109
Checklists, 45, 107
Client, 22
Client's requirements, 25, 30, 117
Close stage, 17, 117
Closure report, 117, 122
Comparative estimate, 26
Consultant, 23
Control, 87
Cost estimates, 25, 51, 101
Costing policy, 26
CPA, 64, 66, 108
Critical path, 75, 109
Critical Path Analysis, 64, 66, 77
Customer, 22

Definitive estimate, 26
Deliverables, 25, 117
Dependency table, 57, 108
Distribution list, 103
Document control, 101

Documenting processes, 53, 101
Duration, 66

End point, 13, 117
Estimating cost, 25
Evaluating change, 99

Feasibility estimate, 26
Filing, 37, 121, 123
Financial authority, 53
Financial performance, 119

Gantt chart, 78, 106, 109

Initiate stage, 17, 18
Issue status, 101

Large sheet plotter, 107
Library, 121
Life cycle, 16, 117
Limiting expenditure, 117
Links, 58
Logic of activities, 57

Matrix organisation, 35
Meeting agenda, 36
Minutes of meetings, 36
Monitoring, 87

Network diagram, 58, 71
Network links, 58

Objectives, 13, 22, 25, 118
Organisation, 35

Paperwork, 121
Personal computer, 106
PERT, 128
Planning process, 82
PRINCE, 128
Procedures, 53, 101
Produce stage, 17
Programme, 13, 28
Progress log, 97
Project manager, 23, 106
Project team, 30, 35

Quality, 15

Relationships, 30
Resources, 81, 109
Retention policy, 123
Review report, 118, 124

Safety, 101

Scheduling, 64
Scope, 25
Selection of Project Manager, 23
Sign off, 117, 122
Site visits, 90
Software, 106
Specify stage, 17, 43
Standard activity box, 65
Start point, 13
Subcontractor, 32

Team meetings, 36, 121
Templates, 107, 113
Time, 15, 64
Total float, 66, 75
Training, 111, 112

Walkabout, 89
Work breakdown structure, 45, 49, 109
Work package, 47

## ORGANISING EFFECTIVE TRAINING
How to plan and run successful courses and seminars

James Chalmers

Industry, public services, colleges, community groups, and organisations of all kinds urgently need to train their people in a wide variety of much needed skills. But however knowledgeable the tutors are, if a training event has been badly organised it will be a waste of everyone's time and money. This book explains how to plan and organise really successful training events. The method can be applied to anything, from team building to technical courses, and from a one hour briefing up to events lasting several days. The step-by-step approach is easy to follow, and will work equally well with organisers who are unfamiliar with the subject to be trained, as well as professional trainers. If you are ever asked to put on an event, or if you want someone to run one for you, then this will give all the necessary guidance and ensure a successful outcome every time. James Chalmers BSc, CEng MIEE has worked in industry for 25 years, and has much experience of running successful training programmes.

*160pp. illus. 1 85703 329 9.*

## CONDUCTING EFFECTIVE NEGOTIATIONS
How to get the deal you want

Patrick Forsyth

Everyone needs to negotiate – whether it's in the office or over the garden fence, buying a car or wage bargaining – it's an everyday activity. Negotiation is the process concerned with striking a bargain and negotiating effectively is a valuable communications skill that anyone can learn. This book sets out in clear practical terms the techniques, the strategies and the ploys of negotiating successfully. You will learn the hidden language of negotiation so that you can recognise what is really going on. This book will show you that negotiation is a manageable process; one that you can control in order to achieve the deal you want. Patrick Forsyth has been in consultancy for over 25 years specialising in communication and management skills, his work has spanned many industries and countries. He is also the author of several successful business books.

*112pp. illus. 1 85703 359 0.*

# How To Books

How To Books provide practical help on a large range of topics. They are available through all good bookshops or can be ordered direct from the distributors. Just tick the titles you want and complete the form on the following page.

___ Apply to an Industrial Tribunal (£7.99)
___ Applying for a Job (£8.99)
___ Applying for a United States Visa (£15.99)
___ Backpacking Round Europe (£8.99)
___ Be a Freelance Journalist (£8.99)
___ Be a Freelance Secretary (£8.99)
___ Become a Freelance Sales Agent (£9.99)
___ Become an Au Pair (£8.99)
___ Becoming a Father (£8.99)
___ Buy & Run a Shop (£8.99)
___ Buy & Run a Small Hotel (£8.99)
___ Buying a Personal Computer (£9.99)
___ Career Networking (£8.99)
___ Career Planning for Women (£8.99)
___ Cash from your Computer (£9.99)
___ Choosing a Nursing Home (£9.99)
___ Choosing a Package Holiday (£8.99)
___ Claim State Benefits (£9.99)
___ Collecting a Debt (£9.99)
___ Communicate at Work (£7.99)
___ Conduct Staff Appraisals (£7.99)
___ Conducting Effective Interviews (£8.99)
___ Coping with Self Assessment (£9.99)
___ Copyright & Law for Writers (£8.99)
___ Counsel People at Work (£7.99)
___ Creating a Twist in the Tale (£8.99)
___ Creative Writing (£9.99)
___ Critical Thinking for Students (£8.99)
___ Dealing with a Death in the Family (£9.99)
___ Do Your Own Advertising (£8.99)
___ Do Your Own PR (£8.99)
___ Doing Business Abroad (£10.99)
___ Doing Business on the Internet (£12.99)
___ Doing Voluntary Work Abroad (£9.99)
___ Emigrate (£9.99)
___ Employ & Manage Staff (£8.99)
___ Find Temporary Work Abroad (£8.99)
___ Finding a Job in Canada (£9.99)
___ Finding a Job in Computers (£8.99)
___ Finding a Job in New Zealand (£9.99)
___ Finding a Job with a Future (£8.99)
___ Finding Work Overseas (£9.99)
___ Freelance DJ-ing (£8.99)
___ Freelance Teaching & Tutoring (£9.99)
___ Get a Job Abroad (£10.99)
___ Get a Job in Europe (£9.99)
___ Get a Job in France (£9.99)
___ Get a Job in Travel & Tourism (£8.99)
___ Get into Radio (£8.99)
___ Getting a Job in America (£10.99)
___ Getting a Job in Australia (£9.99)
___ Getting into Films & Television (£10.99)
___ Getting That Job (£8.99)
___ Getting your First Job (£8.99)
___ Going to University (£8.99)

___ Having a Baby (£8.99)
___ Helping your Child to Read (£8.99)
___ How to Study & Learn (£8.99)
___ Investing in People (£9.99)
___ Investing in Stocks & Shares (£9.99)
___ Keep Business Accounts (£7.99)
___ Know Your Rights at Work (£8.99)
___ Learning to Counsel (£9.99)
___ Live & Work in Australia (£12.99)
___ Live & Work in Germany (£9.99)
___ Live & Work in Greece (£9.99)
___ Live & Work in Italy (£8.99)
___ Live & Work in Portugal (£9.99)
___ Live & Work in the Gulf (£9.99)
___ Living & Working in America (£12.99)
___ Living & Working in Britain (£8.99)
___ Living & Working in China (£9.99)
___ Living & Working in Hong Kong (£10.99)
___ Living & Working in Israel (£10.99)
___ Living & Work in New Zealand (£9.99)
___ Living & Working in Saudi Arabia (£12.99)
___ Living & Working in the Netherlands (£9.99)
___ Living Away From Home (£8.99)
___ Making a Complaint (£8.99)
___ Making a Video (£9.99)
___ Making a Wedding Speech (£8.99)
___ Manage a Sales Team (£8.99)
___ Manage an Office (£8.99)
___ Manage Computers at Work (£8.99)
___ Manage People at Work (£8.99)
___ Manage Your Career (£8.99)
___ Managing Budgets & Cash Flows (£9.99)
___ Managing Credit (£8.99)
___ Managing Meetings (£8.99)
___ Managing Projects (£8.99)
___ Managing Your Personal Finances (£8.99)
___ Managing Yourself (£8.99)
___ Market Yourself (£8.99)
___ Mastering Book-Keeping (£8.99)
___ Mastering Business English (£8.99)
___ Master GCSE Accounts (£8.99)
___ Master Public Speaking (£8.99)
___ Migrating to Canada (£12.99)
___ Obtaining Visas & Work Permits (£9.99)
___ Organising Effective Training (£9.99)
___ Pass Exams Without Anxiety (£7.99)
___ Passing That Interview (£8.99)
___ Plan a Wedding (£8.99)
___ Planning Your Gap Year (£8.99)
___ Preparing a Business Plan (£8.99)
___ Publish a Book (£9.99)
___ Publish a Newsletter (£9.99)
___ Raise Funds & Sponsorship (£7.99)
___ Rent & Buy Property in France (£9.99)
___ Rent & Buy Property in Italy (£9.99)

# How To Books

| | |
|---|---|
| ___ Research Methods (£8.99) | ___ Use the Internet (£9.99) |
| ___ Retire Abroad (£8.99) | ___ Winning Consumer Competitions (£8.99) |
| ___ Return to Work (£7.99) | ___ Winning Presentations (£8.99) |
| ___ Run a Voluntary Group (£8.99) | ___ Work from Home (£8.99) |
| ___ Setting up Home in Florida (£9.99) | ___ Work in an Office (£7.99) |
| ___ Setting Up Your Own Limited Company (£9.99) | ___ Work in Retail (£8.99) |
| | ___ Work with Dogs (£8.99) |
| ___ Spending a Year Abroad (£8.99) | ___ Working Abroad (£14.99) |
| ___ Start a Business from Home (£7.99) | ___ Working as a Holiday Rep (£9.99) |
| ___ Start a New Career (£6.99) | ___ Working in Japan (£10.99) |
| ___ Starting to Manage (£8.99) | ___ Working in Photography (£8.99) |
| ___ Starting to Write (£8.99) | ___ Working in the Gulf (£10.99) |
| ___ Start Word Processing (£8.99) | ___ Working in Hotels & Catering (£9.99) |
| ___ Start Your Own Business (£8.99) | ___ Working on Contract Worldwide (£9.99) |
| ___ Study Abroad (£8.99) | ___ Working on Cruise Ships (£9.99) |
| ___ Study & Live in Britain (£7.99) | ___ Write a Press Release (£9.99) |
| ___ Studying at University (£8.99) | ___ Write & Sell Computer Software (£9.99) |
| ___ Studying for a Degree (£8.99) | ___ Write for Publication (£8.99) |
| ___ Successful Grandparenting (£8.99) | ___ Write for Television (£8.99) |
| ___ Successful Mail Order Marketing (£9.99) | ___ Writing a CV that Works (£8.99) |
| ___ Successful Single Parenting (£8.99) | ___ Writing a Non Fiction Book (£9.99) |
| ___ Survive Divorce (£8.99) | ___ Writing a Report (£8.99) |
| ___ Surviving Redundancy (£8.99) | ___ Writing a Textbook (£12.99) |
| ___ Taking in Students (£8.99) | ___ Writing an Assignment (£8.99) |
| ___ Taking on Staff (£8.99) | ___ Writing an Essay (£8.99) |
| ___ Taking Your A-Levels (£8.99) | ___ Writing & Publishing Poetry (£9.99) |
| ___ Teach Abroad (£8.99) | ___ Writing & Selling a Novel (£8.99) |
| ___ Teach Adults (£8.99) | ___ Writing Business Letters (£8.99) |
| ___ Teaching Someone to Drive (£8.99) | ___ Writing Reviews (£9.99) |
| ___ Travel Round the World (£8.99) | ___ Writing Romantic Fiction (£9.99) |
| ___ Understand Finance at Work (£8.99) | ___ Writing Science Fiction (£9.99) |
| ___ Use a Library (£7.99) | ___ Writing Your Dissertation (£8.99) |

To: Plymbridge Distributors Ltd, Plymbridge House, Estover Road, Plymouth PL6 7PZ. Customer Services Tel: (01752) 202301. Fax: (01752) 202331.

Please send me copies of the titles I have indicated. Please add postage & packing (UK £1, Europe including Eire, £2, World £3 airmail).

☐ I enclose cheque/PO payable to Plymbridge Distributors Ltd for £ _____

☐ Please charge to my ☐ MasterCard, ☐ Visa, ☐ AMEX card.

Account No. ☐☐☐☐☐☐☐☐☐☐☐☐☐☐☐

Card Expiry Date ☐ | 19 | ☎ **Credit Card orders may be faxed or phoned.**

Customer Name (CAPITALS) ...............................................................

Address ...............................................................................

................................................... Postcode ...............

Telephone........................... Signature ...................................

Every effort will be made to despatch your copy as soon as possible but to avoid possible disappointment please allow up to 21 days for despatch time (42 days if overseas). Prices and availability are subject to change without notice.

Code BPA